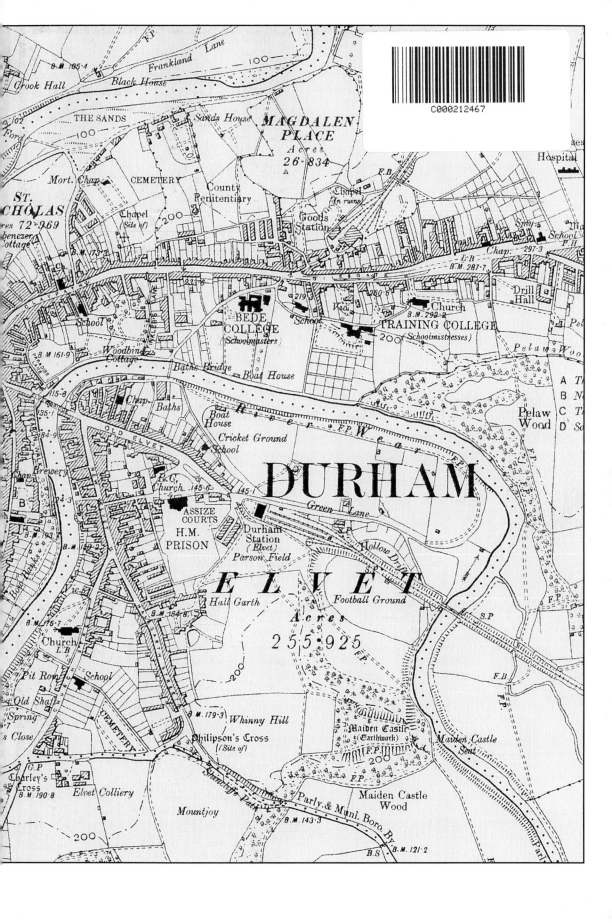

DURHAM CITY

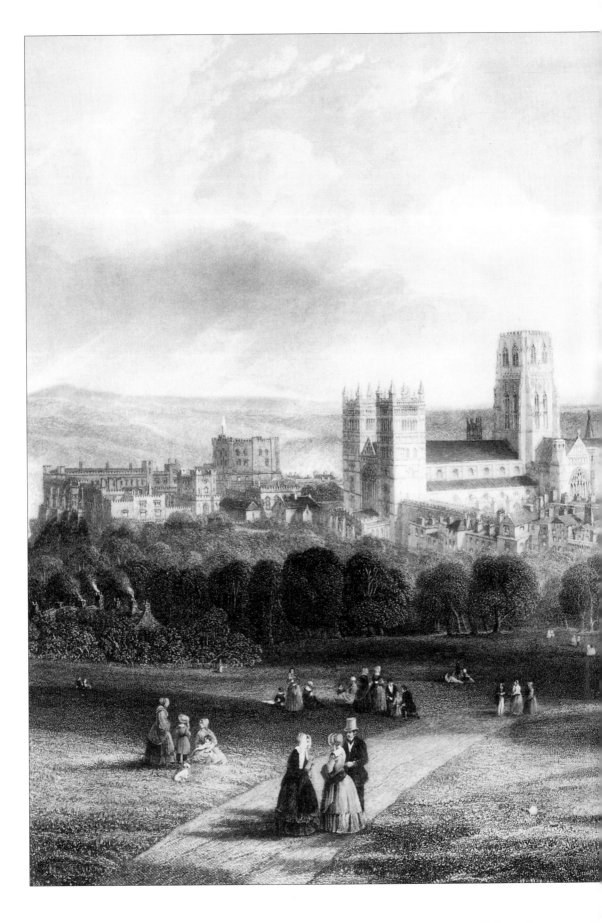

DURHAM CITY

Keith Proud

Phillimore

2003

Published by
PHILLIMORE & CO. LTD
Shopwyke Manor Barn, Chichester, West Sussex, England

ISBN 1 86077 249 8

Printed and bound in Great Britain by
THE CROMWELL PRESS
Trowbridge, Wiltshire

CONTENTS

LIST OF ILLUSTRATIONS

Frontispiece: 'Cathedral and castle from the south-west'

ACKNOWLEDGEMENTS

As the poet John Donne once famously wrote, 'No man is an island, entire of itself'. This book could not have been completed without much-valued assistance from a number of people whose help I gratefully acknowledge.

I would like to thank John Burton for writing the Foreword and for telling me about the Roman mosaic 'somewhere in Trimdon Village'. My old friend Neville Turner has kindly taken most of the photographs in the book. I have consulted works by a number of authors who have all contributed to extending the knowledge we have of Durham City. Ray Selkirk, an archaeologist with an extensive knowledge of the North East, was enormously helpful in providing unpublished information about the Old Durham area. Audrey Thompson, Durham County Council's Information and Local Studies Officer at the city's Clayport Library, worked with her team to help me to find photographs of Durham in former times. The County Archaeologist, Fiona Macdonald, helped with the section of the book dealing with Cade's Road and the findings, at Sedgefield, of the 'Time Team'. Permission to include the map of Durham City was generously given by Martin Boulton, Tourism Officer for Durham City; his staff were also most helpful on a number of occasions.

I am deeply indebted to the Chapter of Durham Cathedral and, in particular, to the Chapter Steward, Anne Heywood, for facilitating my photography in the cathedral, and for so generously allowing me to include a number of their own superb photographs. The numbers of these illustrations are: 11, 12, 13, 15, 16, 17, 19, 20, 21, 43, 44, 45, 46, 48, 49, 50, 51, 52, 53, 71, 72, 73 and 87.

Special thanks must go my editor at Phillimore, Simon Thraves, and to their extremely patient managing director, Noel Osborne, who encouraged and supported me throughout the writing of this book. Peter Cook and Nicola Willmot have also been of constant assistance in its production.

My grateful thanks to all others who have supported this work in any way, and especially to my wife, Barbara, who accompanied me, in frequently inclement weather, on expeditions around Durham City. She has also been invaluable in reading proofs and generally ensuring that I completed this book — which I dedicate to her.

FOREWORD

Durham City is a place which has always been and still is very special to me. There are so many of its constituent elements which merit mention. Its prince bishops, both good and bad, were the principal characters in an almost unbelievable saga which spanned nearly a thousand years. Its architecture is awesome, its narrow streets almost visibly haunted by phantom footfalls from bygone times. Its university continues to cherish a most enviable reputation as a superb seat of learning. Its history reflects, in so many ways, the history of our nation.

Durham City has always been part of my life. As a youngster, I was often taken to the annual Miners' Gala where, I suppose, I first unknowingly encountered aspects of the world of politics, when I heard 'the great and the good' speak from the racecourse platforms. I spent three incredibly happy years here at Bede, one of the finest colleges in the country, training to be a teacher and pursuing my sporting interests. It was from Durham railway station that my wife Lily and I, along with a trusted motor cycle which travelled in the guard's van, set off together to Hertfordshire to start our married life in what we regarded, at the time, as 'the deep south'. Looking across to that famous, familiar view of the cathedral and castle as the train pulled out of Durham station made our departure even more poignant.

Now, so many years later, I am proud to serve as a member of the Council of Durham Cathedral and to have been appointed as one of the Lord Lieutenant's deputies. Acting in these capacities, I trust that, in some small way, I can repay Durham City for the decades of pleasure it has afforded me.

This new book, written by a man who, along with its principal illustrator, Neville Turner, is Durham to the marrow, tells the Durham City story as a detailed yet easily readable narrative. I commend it to you.

John Burton, D.L.,
Constituency Agent to the Rt Hon. Tony Blair M.P.

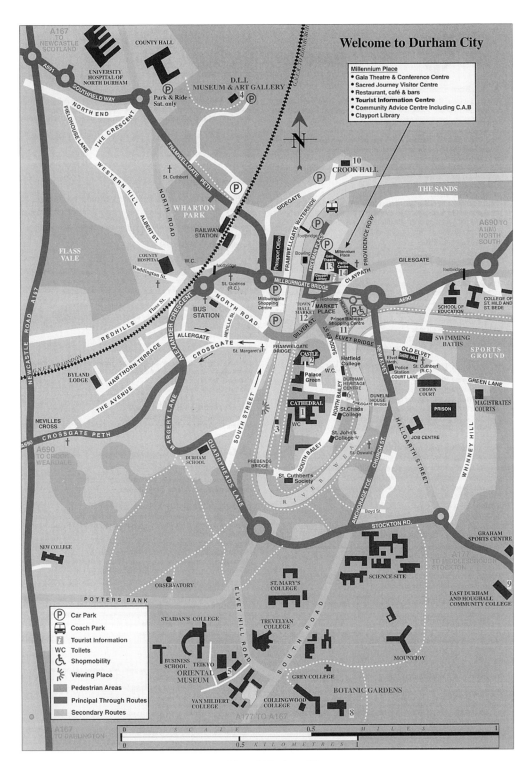

1   *Map of Durham City.*

Introduction

Durham is a magical city, a living chronicle, in microcosm, of the history of England.

Its charm lies in its infinite variety, in its superb blend of architectural styles from medieval to modern, its ability to bewitch visitor and resident alike no matter what the weather or the season. Whether bathed in brilliant sunshine or with its cobbles silvered after rain, new perspectives are continually revealed. Its walkways and greens may be strewn with countless myriad-coloured autumn leaves. When lying under its winter carpet of snow, Durham is transformed into a fairy-tale Christmas land where vegetable vendors ply their trade as they have done across the years in the ancient market place while bankers, barristers and assorted undergraduates bustle about their business, brushing past determined shoppers and ambling tourists who linger here and there, temporarily divorced from reality, haunted by the beauty of the place.

John Speed's 1610 map of the City of Durham carries the description:

> The ancient Citie Duram, by the Saxons called Dunholm, which as Beda sayth is compounded of their two words Dun, an hill, and Holm an island, is in like form and situation as here is described. The first erectors of this Citie are sayde to be the Monks of Lindisferne which by the raging of the Danes were driven thence, and wandrig farre and wyde, at last by oracle (as in those dayes there were maney, if we believe their monkish legende) they were commanded to seat here, about the yere of grace 993 where Cuthbert their Bishop obtained a great opinion of santitye and no less revenews and authoritye.
>
> In the upper part of this Citie, mounted upon an hill, William the Conqueror, for her defence built a strong Castell, and for her profit and pleasure, nature hath girtt her almost round with ye sweet and delectable river of were.

The monks actually arrived in A.D. 995 but the rest of the description will suffice. An Anglo-Saxon poem describes Durham as a 'city celebrated in the whole Empire of the Britons'. Today that fame continues, and rightly so, but now visitors come from all parts of the world as well as from all over Britain itself. Many, it must be said, arrive with a totally inaccurate notion of what the city will be like. They seem to expect a large church and castle surrounded as far as the eye can see by serried ranks of drab, Coronation Street-like terraces, a pall of industrial smoke hanging permanently over them.

Nothing could be further from the truth. Durham City is beautiful, compact and charming to behold as well as being fascinating and interesting in a thousand ways. A cathedral, a castle, a university, ancient schools, bridges, an array of churches, an organ factory, a prison, a market place and some fine public buildings are the principal threads woven into the colourful tapestry which is the City of Durham today.

The first true builders of Durham City were men of the Church but they were not the first inhabitants. The large mound of Maiden Castle stands between Hallgarth Street and Shincliffe village, bearing possible testament to the existence of prehistoric inhabitants in the area, while at Old Durham, about a mile to the east of the market place, remains have been found of a Romano-British farmstead, occupied probably from the second to the fourth centuries. Some finds in Durham City suggest that there were inhabitants on the peninsula before the monks arrived with St Cuthbert's body, probably even before the Roman occupation of Britain. This should not be altogether surprising since the site is readily defensible and would surely have suggested itself as a home to many before the monks.

An area of Durham referred to as 'Aelfet ee', and translated as Elvet Island, is mentioned in the Laud (Peterborough) manuscript of the Anglo-Saxon Chronicle. The entry records that on 17 July in the year A.D. 762 a priest called Peohtwine was there consecrated Bishop of Whithorn in Galloway. Whether this consecration took place in the area now known as Elvet or actually on the peninsula is not known nor is it particularly important, the relevant point being that there was Christian activity in the immediate area of Durham some two centuries before the arrival of Cuthbert's body. Nor was it an isolated event. Nearby at Finchale, synods were held in A.D. 792, 798 and in 810. A few miles south of Durham at Great Aycliffe, synods had taken place in A.D. 782 and 789 and the simple Saxon stone church beside the Wear at Escomb near Bishop Auckland was already built before the end of the seventh century.

To a great many people, Durham's cathedral is the finest example of Norman architecture to be seen anywhere. Its situation is spectacular, its construction brilliant and, standing as it does on its rocky plateau high above the River Wear, it presents the most beautiful aspect. To Sir Walter Scott, Durham Cathedral was 'Half church of God, half castle gainst the Scot', and for centuries it was precisely that. The Scots were rarely away from Durham's doors, led there in battle by kings and chieftains or travelling of their own volition as raiding parties in search of plunder. The paradox was that Durham's very *raison d'être* was the precious body of a Scottish-born monk whose guardians had fled to this place to escape the unwelcome attentions of marauding Vikings. The saint seemed destined never to find a peaceful resting place.

From the time of his death in A.D. 687 until the murder and canonisation of Thomas à Becket in the late 12th century, Cuthbert was England's most famous saint. His monastic career had begun at Melrose, continued at Ripon and ended on the windswept Farne Islands near Lindisfarne, the 'Holy Island' just off the coast of Northumberland. In A.D. 685, he had, reluctantly, accepted the Bishopric of Lindisfarne, relinquishing the post a short time before his death. Cuthbert was buried in the monastery on Lindisfarne and pilgrims were soon travelling to visit his tomb. When, 11 years later, the monks decided that the tomb should be in a more important part of the church and that Cuthbert should be re-interred in a new oak coffin, they found that his body had not decayed at all and that the saint looked as if he were merely sleeping. The story of the miracle of the perfectly preserved corpse spread rapidly and added enor-mously to the saint's prestige. Then even more pilgrims came!

In A.D. 875, continued Viking attacks against Lindis-farne and the Northumbrian coast caused the monks to leave their monastery and to transport Cuthbert's body to a more secure resting place. After many and widespread perambulations, they found refuge at the old Roman settlement of Chester-le-Street where the body remained until A.D. 995 when the monks again

2   *Durham Cathedral and the Fulling Mill from Prebends' Bridge.*

moved to find a safe haven and to escape, it is thought, a renewed threat of Viking incursions. Ripon served briefly as a temporary home and then, so the story goes, as they journeyed back to Chester-le Street, Cuthbert's guardians found that they were unable to move the coffin. It refused to be stirred and no effort on their part was to any avail. The problem was eventually overcome when one of the monks had a vision and the final resting place of the saint was the peninsula of land which was destined to become the City of Durham. The body was eventually housed in the magnificent Norman cathedral.

After William I's conquest of England, the old Saxon defences at Durham were replaced by more sophisticated Norman ones. Precisely how the site was defended before the arrival of the Normans is not known but the conquerors determined that since Durham was such a strategically important site it had to be well guarded. They

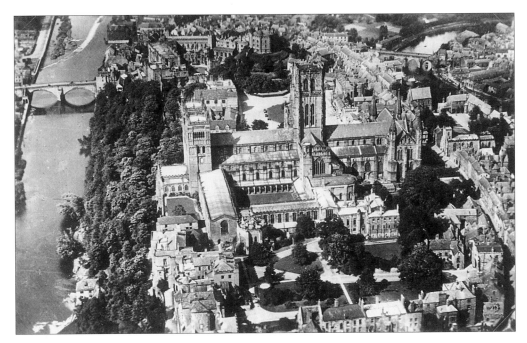

3 *Aerial view of Durham Cathedral from the south.*

erected the castle, first built of wood and later of stone. They constructed wooden
palisades, again later rebuilt of stone to create massive walls around an inner and
outer bailey.

Nor did it take the Norman barons long to realise how important Durham was
politically, situated as it was so close to Scotland, and it was a stroke of pure genius
on the part of the monarch to install as overlord of the area a churchman instead of
a secular baron to safeguard his interests. A bishop would surely never rise up against
his king, whereas others might. Not even the wisest ruler, however, could have
imagined the immense power which would eventually accrue to his Durham
representative.

Around the saint's body there grew what can only be described as the Cult of
Cuthbert. Almost from the body's arrival in Durham, it was visited by kings and
commoners, noblemen, knights and pilgrims in ever increasing numbers and it was
during the Middle Ages that the city reaped the richest rewards from its saintly
patron. This was the era of the great medieval guilds and those in Durham were not
slow to take advantage of the increased trade which came their way several times a
year, notably on St Cuthbert's two feast days in March and September and at
Whitsuntide when great fairs were held at Durham to cater for the huge influx of
pilgrims. The guild members themselves repaid St Cuthbert at the Feast of Corpus
Christi by taking part in the lavish Procession of the Guilds. It was then that they

walked behind their guild banners to the great church to be met by the monks who came out to greet them carrying the supposedly indestructible banner of St Cuthbert. On what is now Palace Green, in front of the cathedral, the guild members performed religious plays, similar to the famous York mystery plays.

The cathedral and monastery continued to grow in stature and in wealth with sub-houses scattered across the north country, but in 1538 Durham suffered at the hands of King Henry VIII and his commissioners during the implementation of the Dissolution of the Monasteries. With the passage of time, however, both cathedral and city recovered from Henry's devastating blow and there arose a new and different hierarchy. The Bishop of Durham was, however, still steadfastly at its head.

4 *The north aisle of the cathedral looking east, engraved by R. W. Billings.*

Durham City today can be a haven of peace where, in many of its quiet places, time truly does seem to stand still, but the city and its environs have had a frequently troubled past. The worst disturbers of the peace were the Scots, who travelled either by the northern route across the Tweed and Tyne or from the west down one of the great river valleys, Weardale and Teesdale being the favoured avenues.

In 1035, King Duncan of Scotland laid siege to Durham but was eventually repulsed and the severed heads of some of his followers were displayed in the market place. In 1071, King Malcolm devastated the eastern part of the bishopric and carried hundreds of Durham folk into captivity in Scotland. In 1136, King David of Scotland invaded the north but was driven back. He tried again, twice, in 1138 but eventually met with a crushing defeat at the Battle of the Standard, fought just to the north of Northallerton in what is now North Yorkshire. Durham City was the venue for a peace conference between the Scottish David and England's King Stephen in 1139.

Such a list of dates and battles, although indicating clearly enough the extent of the damage done to Durham by repeated Scottish incursions, does rather tend to give the impression that there were comparatively long periods of peace punctuated by the occasional act of war. The truth is that, to the people of Durham, the threat of an isolated attack or an all-out Scottish invasion was omnipresent. Vigilance could never be relaxed and recovery of land, economy and population after even a brief period of strife necessitated years of hard work.

In 1174 the Scots attempted yet another invasion under William the Lion but his plans were foiled before his army had travelled far and there followed more than a century of comparative peace for the English north country. Then, in 1312, Robert the Bruce of Scotland crossed the border, ill-defined and fluctuating as it was at the time, and did great damage to the north of England. When he returned in 1313, he travelled with such speed that he was in the outskirts of Durham, burning and pillaging, almost before anyone realised what was happening.

After the Scottish victory at the Battle of Bannockburn in 1314, very few parts of the north escaped the raiding which followed. Stockton-on-Tees was destroyed and the town and port of Hartlepool were ravaged and burned. The famine which ensued was to last for several decades. The hardship suffered by the population of the area is almost unimaginable today. Food of any sort was so scarce that some people resorted to cannibalism and parents had to guard their children in case they were stolen to suffer this most dreadful fate. Throughout Durham, rents were reduced because the people were quite simply unable to find the money or produce to meet their obligations. Some communities were so badly hit by the Scots that they were just abandoned, the survivors moving to live elsewhere. Recovery from the carnage, where any recovery was viable, was extremely slow.

1346 was the year of the Battle of Neville's Cross, fought just outside Durham City. King Edward III was absent from England, laying siege to Calais, when Scotland's David II, at the request of Philip VI of France who wanted a diversion created, led his army into England. Edward, however, remained where he was and his wife, Queen Philippa, journeyed north to meet the Scottish threat, gathering an army as she went. To her aid came the Archbishop of York and the great houses of Neville and Percy. King David was captured during the battle in which the Scots were heavily defeated. He remained a prisoner of the English for 11 years.

Fighting continued intermittently through the succeeding centuries until, in 1650, 3,000 Scots came right into the heart of Durham City but this time the Scots came as captives after the Battle of Dunbar on 3 September. They were imprisoned in the cathedral where the havoc they wreaked on the fabric of the old church was dreadful. To be fair to the Scots, they had not been treated well, were absolutely exhausted, half-starved and many of their number had died on the long march south. Such

5 *A cricket match on the racecourse ground in 1849.*

desperate men can not be blamed for having had scant regard for the building's medieval heritage. They were hungry and they were cold. No fuel was available to them so they kept warm by burning anything they could find, including beautiful medieval woodwork, choir stalls and much else, sparing the wooden clock case, it was said, because of the thistle carved on it. If posterity is to accuse the Scots of vandalism then it must indict their gaolers too, for not only did they rob their prisoners of what little worldly wealth they retained but they despoiled the cathedral by stealing the medieval brass lectern in the shape of a pelican. Thus it can perhaps be seen why the citizens of Durham were so set against the Scots and why members of the city guilds refused for centuries to accept Scotsmen as apprentices to their trades.

It was during Cromwell's time, between the years 1653 and 1656, that the County of Durham first sent representatives to the House of Commons. Attempts had been made to secure this right since the beginning of that century but, because of the power of the Bishop of Durham who so violently opposed the idea, nothing had previously been achieved. Now, with the Bishop removed for the duration of the Commonwealth, the obstacle was gone. Henry Davison was the first member to represent the county, followed, in September 1654, by Robert and George Lilburn and James Clavering. The City of Durham was represented by Alderman Anthony Smith, a mercer, chosen by the freemen of the city.

Oliver Cromwell also succeeded, where many monarchs had tried and failed, in removing almost completely the power, influence and assets of the Bishop of Durham. It was a state of affairs destined not to be permanent but while it existed it condemned the Bishop, Thomas Morton, to poverty, abuse and near oblivion. Almost in his

6   *The cathedral from Framwellgate in 1842, engraved by R. W. Billings.*

stead there was created a parliamentary official, Sir Thomas Haslerigg. He and his family bought prestigious property throughout the county, including the Bishop's Palace at Bishop Auckland which he remodelled to his own taste.

During the bitter Civil War between King Charles I and the English Parliament, it had been almost inevitable that the County of Durham, the intrinsic bishopric, would side with the King. The Puritans had no love for the established Church nor for its bishops and many of the people of the county and city were still predisposed to the old Roman Catholic religion, Puritanism being pure anathema to folk loath to abandon the old ways. Even before the Civil War, in fact, the people of the majority of County Durham supported the King in his war against the Scots.

Charles I had first passed through the bishopric as a child when he followed his father, James VI of Scotland, James I of England, into his new kingdom. The royal children were then the guests of the Bishop of Durham at Auckland Castle. When, in 1633, Charles returned to the county, this time as King, he was entertained at Raby Castle near Staindrop and then again at Auckland Castle before riding in majesty into Durham City. The welcome prepared for him in 1633 was in marked contrast to that he was to receive 14 years later. On the former occasion he was met by the High Sheriff of Durham who was accompanied by an entourage of 200 men along with all the finest gentlemen of the county. Loyal greetings having been delivered, King Charles was accompanied by this great throng to the cathedral. Later that day he lodged at Durham Castle as the guest of Bishop Morton and a dear visit it proved to be, costing the churchman some £1,500 per day. On that occasion the King was on his way to be crowned in Edinburgh.

7   *Durham North Road railway viaduct from the cathedral tower.*

In February 1647, King Charles again passed through Durham but this time there were no welcoming gentlemen, for the King came as the prisoner of the English Parliament. He had been bought from the Scots for the sum of £20,000, a fee which also guaranteed the withdrawal of their army from English soil. The unhappy monarch travelled through the city on his way from Newcastle-upon-Tyne to London, guarded by Parliamentary commissioners. Charles I eventually lost his head and when his son, Charles II, was restored to the throne at the end of the Commonwealth he did nothing to further the cause of a university for Durham. He did not plan to perpetuate what had been a Cromwellian ideal.

During the 18th and 19th centuries, life in Durham City changed. No longer was it under constant threat of invasion. With this new-found stability, building began on a scale not seen in the city for hundreds of years. Graceful terraces rose where city walls had once stood as a necessity. The Baileys ceased to be places of safety and became, instead, fashionable addresses. Durham became a centre of justice with its law courts, a haven of culture with theatres and libraries. Literature flourished while the great and famous came to view and to grace the new order. The cathedral became a sort of Barchester where canons' wives seem, at times, to have wielded as much, if not more, power as the canons themselves. This was the Durham of polite society, a cultured place which attempted to emulate life in Bath or Cheltenham and,

8   *H.R.H. the Prince of Wales, later King Edward VIII, on a visit to Durham.*

as far as can be ascertained, succeeded to a degree in that effort. Durham had no spa but neither Bath nor Cheltenham had a Cuthbert.

In contrast to this way of life, there was also poverty, a scourge which was evident until the Second World War and even afterwards in parts. The miners who came to shop in Durham City must have looked into the windows of some shops and wondered how anyone on earth could have afforded the items on display. There were slums in the city itself, some only demolished in the 1950s. Today much of the city's population lives in pleasant suburbs of good, new housing erected since the mid-20th century. The old road pattern has altered almost beyond recognition and the city centre has been revamped.

Bridging the centuries as easily as its bridges span the river, this, then, is the City of Durham, last resting place of Cuthbert and of the Venerable Bede, one-time home of the notorious prince bishops of Durham and manifestly a city for all seasons.

One

THE DURHAM AREA BEFORE A.D. 995

The peninsula on which the Saxon settlement which grew to become Durham City was founded is one of the finest natural fortifications in Britain. For many people, the history of this place begins with the arrival of St Cuthbert's body in A.D. 995 and almost all documentary evidence about Durham does, indeed, date essentially from that event. However, Durham's story goes back very much further. Historians have long argued that the obvious virtues of such a readily defensible site must surely have been realised by others long before the 'Cuthbert Community' settled here but there is very little tangible evidence to support this contention. Prehistoric people followed by Romans and Saxons have all been present, in their turn, on the peninsula but have left little to mark their passing.

Nevertheless, in attempting to identify the possible origin of any settlement, such indicators as place-names can frequently be of great help. The word *Wear*, the river which flows past Durham and almost surrounds the peninsula, is Celtic in origin and means, simply, *river*. In close proximity to Durham itself, post-Roman but pre-Norman place-names are numerous – Brandon, Bowburn, Coxhoe, Finchale, Newton, Pittington, Rainton, Sherburn, Shincliffe, Ushaw, Willington – as they are across the whole of what is now recognised as County Durham. One of the earliest versions of the city's name, *Dunholm*, suggests an amalgamation of *dun*, meaning *hill*, from Old English and *holmr*, Old Norse for *island* or *cliff*, hence *hill island* or *hill with cliffs*; either interpretation would suit the craggy peninsula. Since the Normans were averse, it seems, to the letter *n* in the middle of words, much preferring an *r*, following their arrival, *Dunholm* gradually evolved into *Durham*.

A considerable amount remains to testify to the Roman occupation of County Durham but comparatively little has been unearthed in and around the city of Durham – fewer than a dozen finds. In 1974, some Roman pottery and one Roman coin of the Emperor Vespasian (A.D. 69-79) were found below some medieval paving in the west range undercroft of the cathedral complex. 1983 and 1985 also saw more pottery fragments unearthed nearby. These finds have been interpreted as being indicative of some form of activity on the peninsula during the Roman period, possibly a native farmstead. Apart from the large number of artefacts in the form of small finds, altars and inscriptions recovered across the county, there are Roman forts including those at Piercebridge, Binchester, Lanchester and Ebchester on Dere Street, the Roman road created between A.D. 78 and 84, which linked York with southern Scotland and passes some seven kilometres to the west of Durham City.

About nine kilometres to the north of the city, on the Roman highway identified by the name of Cade's Road, after John Cade, the 18th-century Darlington-born antiquary, is the Roman fort of Chester-le-Street. Cade's Road, built probably some 60 years (between A.D. 138-161) after Dere Street, ran from Brough on the Humber to a bridging point on the River Tees near Middleton-St-George. It then continued through County Durham via Sadberge, Great Stainton (formerly known as Stainton-le-Street), Sedgefield and Chester-le-Street to the Roman fort at Newcastle-upon-Tyne, the Roman *Pons Aelius*, but its precise course in the area of Durham City has never properly been identified.

The two routes *via* Durham which, in the absence of firm evidence, have been suggested as the most plausible possibilities both pass through or around the area of High Shincliffe to the south of Durham City. One theory is that Cade's Road could have crossed the Wear near to the present Shincliffe Bridge. Such a road could then have passed just to the west of Maiden Castle hill, turned east to the south of Elvet and followed the high ground up to Aykley Heads before traversing Framwellgate Moor and carrying on almost due north to Chester-le-Street. Even more likely is that this elusive road ran to the east of today's Durham City, passed through or very close to Old Durham, through Pelaw, and bridged the Wear only once, probably near Kepier, a route complying more readily with the few clues history has left. Both theories have their advocates and there is even a credible school of thought which reasons that at least two and even three or more Roman roads could have passed across or around the Durham peninsula.

Highly relevant in any consideration as to the most probable routes of Cade's Road are the dates of Maiden Castle, Pelaw, the Roman 'villa' at Old Durham and of early building at Old Durham itself. No firm evidence has yet emerged for the actual date of the construction and occupation, or occupations, of Maiden Castle. During the late 18th and 19th centuries there was much speculation by antiquaries such as Hutchinson, Cade, Stukeley and Surtees about this, but even after some excavation in 1956 no firm date has yet been suggested for the construction of the site, which is now more densely wooded than it was in their day, and its origins remain unclear. However, its naturally defensible position could suggest, depending on interpretation, an Iron-Age fort, a Roman, Dark-Age, early Saxon or Viking settlement, one from the early medieval period or several different occupations.

Cade conformed to the most common interpretation of the name Pelaw as being a corruption of *Pele Law*, a hill on which there was a defended, but more usually medieval tower, remains of one of which he found and which he interpreted as a Roman signal station, its purpose having been to facilitate communication. Further investigation of some of the stones used in the construction of the present Old Durham farmhouse may well suggest that they have been 'removed' from some Roman building, possibly nearby. Cade wrote:

> The ground-plot and ramparts of the watch tower, which served for signals to this station [Old Durham?], are visible and almost entire at the entrance of Gilligate [Gilesgate] Moor, and exactly correspond in form with those on the Roman Wall in Northumberland. At Newton Hall likewise, on the opposite side of the river, there has been an exploratory castrum, seemingly for the security of Old Durham and Chester le Street.

The high ground of Aykley Heads, Framwellgate and the Newton Hall area are excellent vantage points but heavily built on since Cade's time, rendering archaeological exploration difficult. In further support of his suggestion as to the route of the Roman road to the east of Durham, Cade explained:

> A gentleman with whom I am acquainted has carefully surveyed the old road from this place [Old Durham./] by Kepyre [Kepier] hospital, and he assures me, that, in a dry season, the piers of a bridge are obvious in the bed of the river, seemingly of Roman construction.

As if to complicate the issue further for today's researcher, he used an illustration enigmatically entitled 'Camp at Maiden Castle now Old Durham'. The 'camp' bears no resemblance in shape or height to the promontory now known as Maiden Castle. Cade was almost certainly describing a different site from that reported by Stukeley and Hutchinson. Like Cade, another historian, Robert Surtees, also described Old Durham as well as the remains of a bridge, or bridges, but failed to make clear precisely where the first of these crossings was, other than that it was, in his opinion, on the line of this Roman road:

> During the late dry summer, the wooden piers of a bridge over the Wear, leading exactly to the station at Old Durham, were not only visible, but those very piers, left high and dry, were taken up, consisting of long trunks of trees, squared and bored, and mortized together so as to form a strong foundation on each side of the river. At the same time, from the same side of the river, piers of solid masonry were discovered on the north side of the Wear below Kepyer Hospital, confirming, it would seem, the old tradition that a great road passed this way across the Race-ground, and so by Kepyer northwards.

The Roman 'villa' site at Old Durham, some 400 metres south of Old Durham farm, was discovered during quarrying operations soon after the start of the Second World War. It was while digging a small test pit to ascertain the viability of extending their quarrying operations in a northerly direction that workers of the Durham City Sand and Gravel Company Ltd came across some masonry. On 9 April 1940, half of a Roman tile was noticed in it and identified by the Reverend Thomas Romans, Master of nearby Sherburn Hospital, along with Mr Colgrave and Mr Hay. It was part of the core of a wall which had been uncovered. By August 1941, natural weathering of the exposed wall and a little basic archaeology revealed that what had been so fortuitously unearthed by the quarrymen included the lining of a small Roman bath.

The site, much of it by then having fallen into the quarry, of what turned out to be the remaining part of a civilian bath-house, complete with hypocaust, was excavated under the direction of Ian Richmond, the Reverend Romans and R.P. Wright at various times between 1941 and 1943. Given that this part of Britain was at one of the most remote extremities of the Roman Empire, on the edge of civilisation, such a find so far north in the country was rare indeed. Much of the labour for this wartime digging was supplied by students from St John's College, Durham and boys from Durham School. As well as a Roman iron key and fragments of Roman pottery, including some Samian ware, a few small Neolithic flints were found, indicating the previous presence in the area of early man. Following the excavations, the archaeologists concluded that the site had been a homestead, purely native before the Antonine period (A.D. 142-58), which had subsequently become Romanised and the bath-house had been added. The pottery remains supported this theory and suggested that it had existed in its Roman form from the mid-second until at least well into the fourth century. There was no evidence that it had any military origin or purpose.

In March 1948, further remains were found 40 metres north-west of the bath-house. These were a circular walled area some 30 metres in diameter and a small part of another walled and paved area which seemed to have been similar in size but most of which had fallen into the quarry. Again excavation was undertaken, led this time by R.P. Wright and John Gillam. Since all of the stratified pottery found was Romano-British and dated from the middle to late second century, the archaeologists suggested that the buildings had been constructed at that time. Because neither structure appeared ever to have been roofed, the conclusion was drawn that they had been open threshing floors.

In 1951, two further paved areas, discovered during operations to quarry more gravel, were found 40 metres north-east of the site of the two circular pavements. Excavation was again undertaken, when time allowed, between August and November. The larger of the two measured seven metres by one metre with a small adjacent patch just under two metres by one metre. The smaller paved area, some ten metres south-west of the larger one, was three metres long and just over one metre wide. These sites, with their sandstone paving, were interpreted as having been used as 'yards' where stacks of corn could be placed, probably within the farm complex. In the centre of the larger area, one of the 'pavings' was found to be an inverted upper quern stone which, until its usefulness came to an end, would formerly have been one of two used together to grind corn. Fragments of third-century pottery were found in a pit beneath part of this larger area. In their 1952 report on this excavation, Wright and Gillam drew the conclusion that the farmhouse which had probably been near the bath-house must have been quarried away before 1940.

How many such farmsteads existed during the second century in what used to be regarded as an almost purely militarised zone of Roman Britain is not known, nor is the spread or density of the civilian population. It may, therefore, be useful to record here that in the early 1950s a builder working in Trimdon village, a few miles to the south-east of Durham, reported to the secretary of the parochial church council that, during the course of some work he had carried out on a house there, he had uncovered part of a Roman mosaic but had covered it over again as, financially, he could not afford to have the job stopped while archaeologists investigated.

In April 2002, an area bordering part of Cade's Road to the west of Sedgefield, a few miles south of Trimdon village, was investigated by television's 'Time Team' programme. The site had been photographed from the air and finds there of Roman pottery and other artefacts were reported by local people. The land was bought by Durham County Council with grant aid from the Heritage Lottery Fund. County Archaeologist Fiona Macdonald worked with the programme's 20 archaeologists while local people undertook field walks. Only three days were available for the excavation. The initial geophysical survey seemed to show a double-ditched trackway with a set of linear enclosures, marked by clear boundaries, as well as other features. Once digging began, quite complex sets of ditches were revealed with dating evidence in the form of second-century pottery. Boundaries of the plots abutting the trackway were clearly visible on the survey. The ditches beside the track were excavated but no metalled road surface was found. Evidence for some of the activities which had been carried out on the site in Roman and later times was unearthed. It seemed as though copper, bronze and glass were worked here and a large, circular, well-preserved pottery kiln was discovered with fragments of pottery still inside it. Because this pottery was of good quality and well made, there was speculation that it had been made for a market such as the Roman military, particularly those who used this road, and, because there was little evidence of buildings, that the site had been used by local natives on an occasional basis for manufacture and trading.

Relevant to any discussion about the lines of Roman roads in and around Durham City is conjecture as to the exact course of a probable link route (and there were, arguably, several), a known Roman road which, just to the north of Willington, branched off from or, more likely, crossed Dere Street in a north-westerly direction through Brancepeth and on to a probable junction or intersection with Cade's Road somewhere in the area north or north-east of Durham City. The suggestion that this link road, before reaching the Durham peninsula, veered north towards Newcastle is highly unlikely since it would then have run not only parallel with but virtually beside Cade's Road. A modern observer, knowing the topography of the county and looking at a map showing the sections of this Willington/Brancepeth Roman road which have been firmly identified, could readily, and logically, surmise that, having crossed the river further to the south at Witton-le-Wear, where the present 'old' bridge dates from 1778, it went on to pass along the ridge to the north-east of Crook and continued until it met Cade's Road in the area to the north of Durham City or continued on across it to a Roman settlement in the area of modern Sunderland near the mouth of the Wear. Another likelihood particularly relevant to the 10th-century development of Durham is that a Roman road from Weardale joined this road. In the absence of actual evidence on the ground, this can still only be conjecture.

What is certain is that across the whole of Roman Britain there was a far more complex network of Roman roads, some better constructed than others, than is currently either known or generally acknowledged. A cursory look at any map of the region, indeed of any part of Britain, readily suggests that the architects and 'navigators' of 18th- and 19th-century wagonways, railways and roads did not fail to grasp the opportunity to make life easier for themselves by utilising routes and solid foundations already in place. Similarly, an argument can be made that many English farms must stand on sites which were once Celtic farmsteads and which have been in almost continuous occupation and use for two thousand years or more.

By the early years of the fifth century, after almost four hundred years of Roman occupation, the British were coming to terms with the fact that Rome had left them to their own devices, the legions having been withdrawn by A.D. 407 and all help from Rome having ceased by A.D. 410. Since the middle of the fourth century, the north of the country had endured incursions by the Picts and the Scots and, later, by the Saxons. The Anglo-Saxon attacks, conquests and gradual colonisation spread to the rest of what is now England, slowly removing and possibly sometimes absorbing, as they gathered momentum, what remained of the Romano-British way of life, its traditions, values and beliefs.

Religion in Roman Britain had been in a state of flux at least since the second century when Christianity seems first to have become established here, probably by Roman soldiers who had encountered it during service in other parts of the empire. Little is known of early Christian activity and organisation in Britain, much being ascribed to the realms of legend. The religion may even have been introduced as early as the middle of the first century A.D. but persecution of Christians across the Roman world did not end officially until A.D. 311. Then, in A.D. 313, Christianity was made legal and in A.D. 314 three British bishops or church leaders, said to have been of London, York and possibly Lincoln, along with a priest and a deacon, reportedly attended the Council of Arles, an important gathering of continental churchmen. There was, then, by that time obviously some form of order to the British Christian tradition, although how extensive or how old any such organisation was is not known. By A.D. 380, Christianity had become not simply legal but also the official religion of the Roman Empire.

The Anglo-Saxon invaders were not Christians but Christianity existed continuously in pockets in different parts of the British Isles throughout the fifth, sixth and seventh centuries. When St Augustine arrived here from Rome with his band of missionaries in A.D. 597, it is said to have been because 'a rumour had reached Rome that the pagan inhabitants of Britain were ready to embrace the faith in great numbers, if only preachers could be found to instruct them'. Pope Gregory was well aware of the existence of the British Church but appears to have believed that it was 'lacking in episcopal zeal'. There were differences in the beliefs and practices of the British, or Celtic, and Roman Christian traditions and Gregory may well have been looking for a way of exerting Roman influence in these islands; an excuse, as it were, for regaining a foothold here for the Church of Rome. Augustine was told by Gregory, in a letter, that he was to have no authority over the

9   *Cathedral stonemason continuing an ancient tradition.*

churches of Gaul but that 'all the bishops of Britain' were entrusted to him in order that 'the unlearned may be instructed, the wavering strengthened by persuasion and the perverse corrected with authority'.

A meeting, which ended acrimoniously, was arranged at Malmesbury between Augustine and the British bishops of the south of the country. The Britons would not give ground on the way the Celtic Church calculated the date of Easter nor on how it conducted baptisms, and felt that it could not work with Augustine on the conversion of the Anglo-Saxons. A subsequent meeting made no more progress, the British bishops finding it impossible to defer to Augustine's wishes simply because he was the Pope's representative in the country. They also regarded him as arrogant but Augustine and his band, unhindered by the lack of co-operation, as they perceived it, from the Celtic Christians, persevered with their mission.

The beginnings of what proved to be an unbroken link between Christianity in Roman Britain and the cathedral which would be built some five hundred years later on Durham's peninsula had already been firmly established. Its originator was a Christian missionary whose name is absent from most history books but to whom a great many churches in Scotland are dedicated. He was Ninian. Born of a British father, possibly of high status, sometime between A.D. 350 and 360, he was baptised a Christian early in his life. The place of his birth was probably Galloway in the south-west of Scotland and in about A.D. 397 he built a church there at Whithorn, the *Candida Casa*, the White Church, and, soon afterwards nearby, a monastery, almost certainly the first in the British Isles. Before doing any of this building, in A.D. 385 he is said to have walked more than 2,000 kilometres to Rome, a journey which took him six months. Before leaving there at the end of his studies, he was consecrated a bishop and sent back to his native Scotland as a Christian evangelist. On his return journey to Britain, he is believed to have paused for a time in Gaul to visit St Martin's monastery at Tours. Ninian was fascinated by the monastic way of life he experienced in France and brought with him to Whithorn stonemasons from Martin's monastery. The Whithorn church and monastery were stone buildings, the church coated externally with plaster or some sort of lime or whitewash so that it was readily visible.

Ninian's name is today not nearly as well known as those of Patrick, Columba, Augustine or Paulinus, yet he was one of the most important Christian bridges between Roman and post-Roman Britain. His missionary work is believed to have taken him and his monks to many parts of southern and eastern Scotland before his death in A.D. 432. Some of his pupils subsequently travelled to Ireland to carry on his work. One of these was Finnbarr, or Finnian, who, later in his life, at the monastic school at Moville, taught Columba, whose work is another link in the Durham story. Columba was born in Ireland in A.D. 521. After spending time in several monasteries and becoming a priest, he travelled with 12 companions in A.D. 563 to the small and remote island of Iona, just off the south-west coast of the much larger Isle of Mull, which itself lies across the firth from Oban on the west coast of Scotland. Here they established a simple monastic settlement. Columba spent most of the rest of his life preaching Christianity and, meeting with no little opposition as he did so, to the people who lived in northern Scotland. He also continued to exercise considerable authority in Ireland.

After his death in A.D. 597, others carried on his teaching at the Iona monastery as well as his missionary work on the mainland and it was to Iona that, in about A.D. 630, an Irish priest came to learn the Columban ways. He was Aidan, a man who would ultimately become one of the north's most famous saints and who would do so much to spread the Christian message in the wild north of a battle-scarred Northumbria. When, at the request of King Oswald, he travelled from Iona to Northumbria in A.D. 635, Aidan must surely have known of an earlier journey made to this northern kingdom just ten years before, not by a Celtic missionary but by Paulinus, one of Augustine's Roman band from Kent.

Paulinus had arrived in Britain in A.D. 601, sent with three others by Pope Gregory to support Augustine's mission. He worked almost exclusively in Kent until A.D. 625 when he was consecrated bishop by Justus, the Archbishop of Canterbury, and accompanied the Christian Ethelburga, sister of King Eadbald of Kent, on her journey to marry the pagan King Edwin of Northumbria. At first the missionary met with very little success but then, at Easter in the year after his arrival in the north, a messenger from Wessex tried unsuccessfully to assassinate King Edwin, and, in gratitude for the fact that his life had been spared, he gave permission for his newly-born daughter to be baptised a Christian, a ceremony she underwent with 11 other members of the royal establishment at Pentecost in A.D. 626. As for Edwin, he was himself baptised by Paulinus at Easter A.D. 627 in a chapel where York Minster now stands. Where the king went his subjects followed and what he did they did. He went to his palace at Yeavering in the Cheviot Hills in Northumberland and with him went his queen and Paulinus. During 36 days, the missionary baptised over three thousand people. He also conducted mass baptisms in the River Swale near Catterick and in other parts of Yorkshire. Then, in A.D. 633, he, the queen and the royal children had to flee back to the south when two powerful pagan kings, Penda and Cadwalla, joined forces to attack Northumbria, killing Edwin at the Battle of Hatfield Chase. Unaware of these events and delighted by what he had heard of Paulinus' success in Northumbria, Pope Honorius created him Archbishop of York – but he never saw that place again.

Aidan was not a fluent speaker of Anglo-Saxon when he arrived in Northumbria but had a strong personality and a persuasive manner. He used interpreters, including the king, to speak to the people and chose as his base the semi-island of Lindisfarne. Twice every day the tide came in and cut it off from the mainland so that there was a kind of solitude and yet at the same time Aidan could still see King Oswald's castle at Bamburgh. On Lindisfarne, Aidan built a monastery which became an important seat of learning and a training ground for the many who followed in his footsteps. One night in A.D. 651, a young shepherd called Cuthbert was working beside the River Leader in Scotland when he saw a soul being taken up to heaven by a group of angels. A few days later, word reached the area that Aidan had died. Soon afterwards, it is said, Cuthbert decided to dedicate his life to God's work.

Two

CUTHBERT – THE SHEPHERD SAINT

Who, then, was this man whose life and miracles attracted enormous interest and around whose supposedly perfectly preserved body the city of Durham was founded? So much has been written over so long a period of time about the man that it is often extremely difficult to separate fact from fiction. The early writers were themselves uncertain about the facts, one going so far as to confuse Cuthbert with another saint and perhaps with more than one. There are, quite literally, hundreds of stories and legends about Cuthbert; so many, in fact, that providing evidence for their veracity is almost impossible. People will believe what they wish about the saint, about his miracles and of the cult which arose after his death.

Cuthbert was probably born in about A.D. 634. Many of the later monks of Durham believed that he was of royal Irish descent. It is probable that they were confusing Cuthbert's birth with that of St Molocus. The Venerable Bede, born during Cuthbert's lifetime and writing within 50 years of the saint's death, does not even refer to the man's birth nor to his earliest origins, starting his account of the life with boyhood in Scotland. Most of the tales of Cuthbert's early life are set in southern Scotland, many of them near Melrose and in the Lammermuir Hills. One of the stories told about him as a boy describes how on one occasion during his childhood, Cuthbert was visited, so the story goes, by an angel. For weeks he had been suffering with a sore knee and was unable to rise from his bed which had been placed outside the cottage so that he could enjoy the sunshine. He was roused from his sleep to discover that a stranger on horseback had approached. As was usual and customary at that time, Cuthbert offered him hospitality. It was obvious to the stranger, however, that the boy could barely move. Dismounting from his horse, he examined Cuthbert's knee and suggested that he should apply a hot wheat poultice to it. This he did and a few days later was up and about, thanks to the advice of an angel, for it was popularly believed later that the horseman had been exactly that. When the bones of Cuthbert were examined many centuries later in Durham Cathedral it was noted that the man interred in the tomb had once suffered from tuberculosis.

Some stories tell how Cuthbert was, at one point, a soldier and others relate how, a few days after the death of Aidan, he decided to become a monk. Bidding farewell to his foster mother, Kenswith, he and a companion rode to the monastery at Melrose. As he approached, out rushed the prior, Boisil, shouting, 'Behold the servant of the Lord'. Cuthbert was admitted to the order and lived and learned at Melrose for six or seven years. Then the abbot, Eata, was made a gift of more land, near Ripon, on which the king wished to see a new monastery built. A band of the Melrose monks, including Cuthbert, went off to start the work. He was to be guestmaster of the new foundation, his primary duty being to ensure that all visitors to the monastery were treated hospitably and that all of their needs were met. Unfortunately, Eata fell soon afterwards from the king's favour and the monks had no option but to return to Scotland.

In 664, the year of the Synod of Whitby at which it was decided that the English church would follow the ways of the Roman and not the Celtic Church, a plague struck the monastery at Melrose and caused devastation. Eata was by then Abbot of Lindisfarne, where he lived, as well as of Melrose but Boisil was still with Cuthbert, now in his 30th year, at Melrose. These last were struck down and the other monks feared the plague would claim their lives too, but Cuthbert recovered. Boisil was not so fortunate and, after a short period during which he predicted that Cuthbert would one day become a bishop, he died. When the effects of the plague eventually passed, Cuthbert tried to continue his work of teaching at the monastery but found the constraints of doing only that too much for him. He needed a new challenge and so he began to travel to villages away from Melrose, the more distant the better. Before long his reputation as a fine speaker preceded him and if there was not a large crowd when he arrived at a place, there was by the time that he left.

Cuthbert's journeys took him further and further away from his Melrose base so that he was sometimes absent from the monastery for many weeks. He would occasionally call at religious houses like the priory at Coldingham, a few miles to the north of Berwick. The abbess there, Ebba, sister to King Oswy, was one of his greatest friends. St Abb's Head, a landmark a stone's throw up the coast from Coldingham, is named after her. Cuthbert is often portrayed as a mysogynist, a hater of women, whereas he had, in fact, many female friends. On one of his visits to Coldingham, an incident occurred which resulted in a story, with several variations, being handed down to posterity. Several times, it was said, Cuthbert, having waited until everyone else in the priory was asleep, rose from his bed and made his way to Coldingham shore, a beautiful expanse of sandy beach. He then waded into the sea until the bitterly cold waves washed around his waist. There he remained for the rest of the night, praying and offering thanks to God for His kindness. As the dawn came up, he walked out of the sea and fell to his knees on the beach, at which point two otters, or seals, depending on which version of the tale is being related, also emerged from the waves, rubbing themselves against his legs and feet to provide him with much-needed warmth after his nocturnal vigil. Unknown to Cuthbert, however, one of the monks from Coldingham had watched all one night from the higher ground, suspicious of Cuthbert's movements. Why, after all, was he abroad when the rest of the community was asleep? Later the next day he confessed to Cuthbert what he had done and begged forgiveness for doubting the man from Melrose. This forgiveness Cuthbert readily granted but instructed him to reveal nothing of what he had seen until after his, Cuthbert's, death.

Cuthbert lived and worked at Melrose for 13 years and then Eata asked him to become Prior of Lindisfarne, so he went to the remote Northumbrian outpost, teaching the monks the new way of monastic life decreed by the Synod of Whitby. These were not just the rules set down by a monk called Benedict who had lived in Italy 200 years earlier but also those of Columba. Obedience, poverty and chastity were the tenets which Benedict had decreed to be the essentials of a Christian monastic life, while Columba's rules were even more strict. Not unnaturally, the monks of this semi-island did not like the proposed new ways and argued daily at the meeting of the chapter against their implementation. If he tired of the controversy, Cuthbert never lost his temper, simply retiring quietly from the meeting. On his return to the forum the following day, he always behaved as if there had never been any dissension and explained yet again his reasons for wishing the community to adopt the new regime. At last his perseverance won the day and the monks eventually accepted his will. There was, after all, something to be said for a way of life which produced a man of the character of Cuthbert. Why was it, they asked themselves, that he never lost his temper and was always cheerful even under the most extreme pressure?

While Cuthbert was Prior of Lindisfarne, Eata, though still based on Lindisfarne, was created Bishop of northern Northumbria. At about the same time, Cuthbert felt the need more and more for the sort of solitude which could be found only in such remote places as the Farne Islands, a group of scattered black rocks which lie off the coast of Northumberland. So, after 12 years as Prior of Lindisfarne, and with a desire to be even nearer to God, Cuthbert sought the haven of those islands. The nearest to the mainland is Inner Farne, some 16 acres in extent, barren and with little grass or vegetation but populated by tens of thousands of seabirds. This was where Cuthbert decided to settle. When he arrived on the island, he was, reportedly, 'beset by demons' but drove away these 'evil spirits' and set about the serious business of creating a shelter for himself. His materials were nothing but stones and soil and his wall was high enough so that all he could see from within it was the sky.

One of the most serious problems Cuthbert had on Inner Farne was finding a supply of drinking water but help was to hand from his friends on Lindisfarne. They rowed across to the island and dug a well for him inside his high wall, Cuthbert praying, as they worked, that water would be found. His prayers were answered. The Lindisfarne monks also helped in the building of a shelter for the many visitors who came to see Cuthbert. For some time, all of his food was rowed across from Lindisfarne but Cuthbert wanted to be totally self-sufficient. He cultivated a patch of ground into which he sowed wheat seed. The crop failed but, not so easily deterred, the following year he planted barley and that was successful.

During these three years on the island, many people came to meet Cuthbert and he greeted them in the guest house, allowing nobody inside his own wall. Gradually he became increasingly reclusive, speaking to visitors only through a hole in the wall through which food was also passed to him once he had given up tending his crops. There was at least one occasion, however, when Cuthbert left the island and that was to travel not to Lindisfarne but to Coquet Island, some way south down the Northumbrian coast. He made the journey to meet his friend Elfled, Abbess of Whitby. Coquet Island was selected as a convenient venue since neither of the two felt able to journey the full distance. At this meeting Cuthbert again expressed his concern that he would soon be asked to become a bishop, and not long afterwards that call came.

10 *Stained glass window in west wall of the cathedral depicting St Cuthbert.*

In A.D. 685, a meeting of Church leaders chose Cuthbert to be Bishop of Hexham but when the news was brought to him he practically ignored the messengers and their letters. For weeks he prevaricated until the situation demanded forthright action.

The king himself, with a large band of important retainers and churchmen, sailed from the Northumbrian coast to Cuthbert's island and Cuthbert came out from behind his walls to meet his visitors. As he approached, they fell to their knees, beseeching him to submit to the request he had so long dreaded. Although he did, eventually, agree to their wishes, he managed to defer his appointment for several months and when he did become a bishop he refused to wear anything other than his simple monk's robes. Hexham was a long way from the Farnes, a fact which obviously troubled Cuthbert, so Eata asked him to come to see him at Melrose. An exchange was agreed. Eata would take the bishopric of Hexham in order that Cuthbert could be Bishop of Lindisfarne in his stead. Although Cuthbert undertook the duties required of him as a bishop, he still found time to travel to some of the loneliest outposts of his see to preach the word of God.

Cuthbert was 51 when he had a premonition that his death was near. He had been bishop for just two years when he resigned the office and returned to Inner Farne. Now, however, he was not so much of a recluse. When the monks visited him from Lindisfarne he emerged to talk to them, but after two months he became ill. The Abbot of Lindisfarne, Herefrith, crossed the short stretch of water to beg him to return to the comparative comfort of Holy Island but Cuthbert would have none of it. He told Herefrith that nearby, when the time was right, would be found a coffin in which he wished to be buried. Herefrith returned with the news to the monastery where for five days he led the monks in prayer for Cuthbert. When a party crossed again to Inner Farne, they found Cuthbert waiting for them in the little guest house. In all that time he had eaten just half an onion. He asked to be helped back to his own hut where, very soon afterwards, he died.

Cuthbert had wanted to be buried on Inner Farne but the monks begged him to let them, instead, take his body to Lindisfarne. He allowed them to have their way but only on condition that, if ever Lindisfarne and its monastic life were threatened in any way, they would take his bones with them when they fled. The body was washed and wrapped first in linen and then in a wax cloth to preserve it before it was moved to the monastery. It was then rowed back to Holy Island where it was buried in a stone coffin to the right of the altar in the monastery church. The year was A.D. 687.

Three

THE CUTHBERT CULT

Although Cuthbert was dead, he was not forgotten. Stories soon began to circulate about people who had been cured of their ailments simply by visiting his burial place. Naturally, as word spread, more and more people came to see if the saint could reach from beyond the grave to help them too. It was not unusual at that time for an important person's bones to be exhumed, washed and reburied. Some 11 years after Cuthbert's death, in A.D. 698, the monks decided to accord him this honour. When they uncovered and opened the coffin, however, they were amazed to find the body looking as it must have done at death. Cuthbert appeared, they reported, as if he were simply asleep. Having made these findings known to their bishop, they disturbed as little as possible and placed the body in a new coffin. This time it was kept above ground.

Still Lindisfarne continued to attract pilgrims, now in greater numbers than before, but in A.D. 793 the island had its first visit from some very unwelcome visitors. Danish Vikings ransacked the church and killed some of the monks. In A.D. 794, there was another Viking raid, this time so great that the monks fled for their lives, leaving behind Cuthbert's body. When they returned they found that, although the rest of their treasures had gone, Cuthbert's tomb had not been touched. There was then a long period of comparative peace until, in A.D. 875, the Danish raiders returned. The monks again had no choice but to leave Lindisfarne and this time they heeded the promise which had been made to the dying Cuthbert and took with them not only his body and his coffin but also some other precious relics, the head of King Oswald, some of

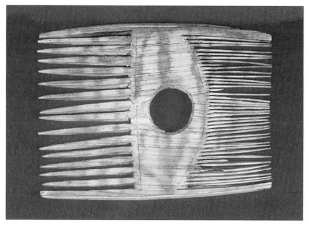

11 *Ivory comb, possibly 11th-century, found in St Cuthbert's tomb.*

25

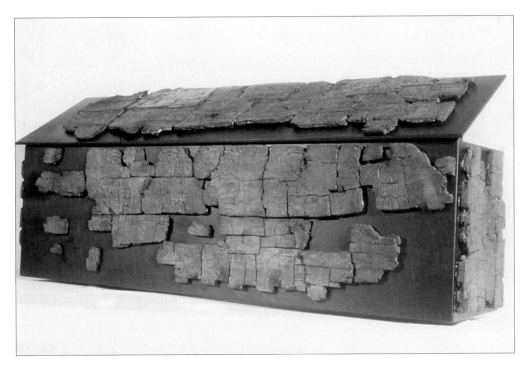

12   *St Cuthbert's coffin, seventh-century.*

13   *Tenth-century stole.*

St Aidan's bones and those of
Eata. Several of the islanders
heard that the monks were
leaving and joined their train.
Although they may have guessed
that they might be absent from
Lindisfarne for some time, the
monks could not possibly have
foreseen that they were destined
to travel about with the coffin
for seven long years, resting in
many places before settling first
at Chester-le-Street and then at
Durham. Wherever they arrived
with the cart bearing the coffin
and other relics, these original
Haliwerfolc, the 'people of the

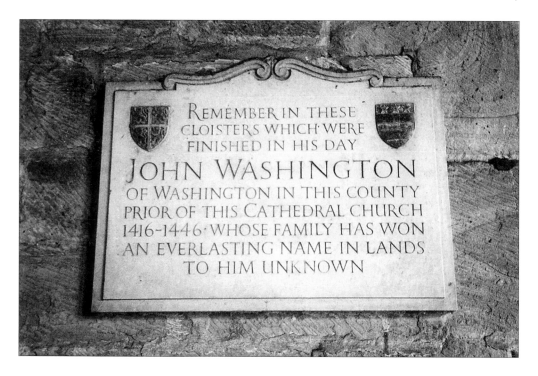

14 *Memorial in the cathedral cloisters to John Washington (de Wessington).*

saint', a title by which, within a century, all who lived in the region were proud to
be known, were met with kindness and, more often than not, with gifts. Cuthbert's
fame, in life and death, had reached into even the most remote fastnesses of the area.
However large the saint's retinue, and numbers must have fluctuated over the years,
only seven of the monks were allowed to touch the coffin, or shrine, and the cart
on which it was transported. At a later date, a horse was procured to relieve the
monks of all the pushing and pulling.

John de Wessington, Prior of Durham in the early 15th century and a gifted
scholar, compiled an itinerary of the places he thought had been visited by the
guardians of Cuthbert's shrine, his research based largely on churches dedicated to
St Cuthbert. In Northumberland he found six, in Westmorland one, in Cumberland
four, in Lancashire eleven. Yorkshire had three, Richmondshire five, the Tees area
of North Yorkshire seven and in Durham there were four. In the early 19th century,
James Raine, historian and friend of Robert Surtees, and editor of a volume of that
writer's monumental *History of Durham*, consulted Wessington's research and
reconstructed what he considered to be the route taken by Cuthbert's guardians.

Having left Lindisfarne, they travelled to Doddington, Elsdon, Bellingham and
Haydon Bridge and then made their way along the course of the South Tyne to
Beltingham. This was followed by a journey along part of Hadrian's Wall and so to

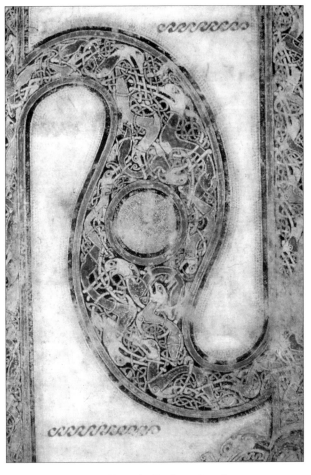

15   *From the Durham Gospels.*

16   *From the Durham Gospels.*

Bewcastle and Carlisle. Salkeld was the next halt, then Edenhall and on to Plumbland. Burnsall, Middleton, Halsall, Lytham, Hambledon, Kellet, Furness, Aldingham, Kirkby Ireleth and Hawkshead took them on a convoluted loop into the Lake District. Still they did not feel safe and considered that they would be well advised to cross to Ireland. They made their way to Workington where a ship was readied, the body and treasures put aboard and, with many monks left on the bank, space being so very limited, the vessel sailed. It did not, however, go very far. A storm arose of such ferocity that the monks rapidly concluded when it ceased that Cuthbert had no desire to be transported to the Emerald Isle.

It was during this storm, it is recorded, that their jewel-adorned volume of the Lindisfarne Gospels was lost overboard. When it was later learned that the book had miraculously turned up at Whithorn, home some 500 years earlier to St Ninian who had founded *Candida Casa* there, along with a Christian church and school, the Cuthbert procession headed north. Their book retrieved, the monks went across the bleak Pennines via Cliburn and Dufton down Teesdale, stopping, it could be argued, at Cotherstone

[Cuthbert's Stone], then on to Marske near Richmond, to Forcett and South Cowton. The next stage took them through Barton, Overton, Fishlake and Ackworth before a huge stride north-east to Kildale, Middleton, Marton, Ormesby, Wilton and Kirkleatham, as if they were heading for the vast mouth of the River Tees, but they would find no easy crossing point there. Back they moved, inland to Redmarshall, near the modern Stockton-on-Tees, then north to Chester-le-Street, the old Roman fort.

After a sojourn at Chester-le-Street of 113 years and the passage of several generations of monks and their camp followers, the guardians were again forced, by renewed Danish activity, to speed south, this time to Ripon. Their stay there was brief indeed and it was while attempting to return to Chester-le-Street that the spirit of St Cuthbert indicated

17 *From the Durham Gospels.*

the place where he wanted them to settle. The man who had led the monks and their treasures to Ripon was Bishop Aldhun, the last true guardian of Chester-le-Street and the monk destined to become the first Bishop of Durham. Earlier in his life, he had been tutor to King Edward the Confessor.

There are numerous stories of how Durham came to be selected but one revolves around a lost cow and either one or two women. As the monks were at *Wrdelau* (Warden Law?), a hill between Houghton-le-Spring and the coastal village of Seaham, which itself has Cuthbertian connections, they found that they were unable to move the cart carrying the shrine. It remained immovable for three days during which time one of the monks, Eadmer, had a vision of St Cuthbert in which he was told that the remains should be taken to Dunholm. This information he relayed to the rest of the party. The problem was that nobody knew where this Dunholm was. It was then

18   *The dun cow panel on the exterior of the cathedral's north wall.*

that two young girls passed the place where the cart was stuck. One was asking the other if she had seen her lost brown cow. She most certainly had, she said. It was across at Dunholm. It had strayed a long way from Warden Law!

The chronicler Symeon, precentor of the monastery at Durham, does not mention the lost cow at all although he does relate how the cart refused to move. In his *A History of the Church of Durham* which he wrote or edited between 1104 and 1108 he explains how:

> the vehicle, on which the shrine containing the holy body was deposited, could not be induced to advance any further. They who attempted to move it were assisted by others, but their efforts, though vigorous, were equally ineffective; nor did the additional attempts of the crowd which now came up produce any result in moving it; for the shrine containing the uncorrupted body continued where it was, as firmly fixed as if it were a mountain. This circumstance clearly intimated to all that he refused to be reconducted to his former place of residence; but at the same time they did not know where they should deposit him, for the place on which they were at that time standing, in the middle of a plain, was then uninhabitable. Hereupon the bishop addressed the people, and gave directions that they should solicit an explanation of this sign from heaven by a fast of three days duration, which should be spent in watching and prayer, in order that they might discover where they should take up their abode along with the holy body of the father. This having been done, a revelation was made to a certain religious person named Eadmer, to the purport that they were required to remove the body to Durham, and there to prepare a resting-place for it. When this revelation was publicly announced,

all were comforted thereby, and joyfully returned thanks to Christ; and a very few of their number were now able to raise the saint's shrine, whereas the whole multitude had previously been unable even so much as to move it. And thus with joy and thanksgiving they translated the holy body to Durham.

So, as the monks set off to find Dunholm, the cart moved easily and it was not long before they arrived at the appointed place, a piece of high ground surrounded by a great loop in the River Wear. The site was 'strong by nature, but not easily rendered habitable, as it was overgrown by a thick forest. In the midst was a small plain, which had been used in tillage.'

   Once the word was put about that Cuthbert's remains were at Durham, people travelled from all parts of the area to help the monks with the business of clearing the site. The first job for Cuthbert's guardians was to erect a shelter for the shrine, 'a little church built quickly of rods'. This they did and next they built a more permanent wooden church, the 'White Church'. Symeon wrote:

> When the whole assembly of the people accompanied the holy body of the father Cuthbert into Durham, it was discovered that the place, although naturally strong, was not easily habitable; for the whole space, with the sole exception of a moderate-sized plain in the midst, was covered with a very dense wood. This had been kept under cultivation, having been regularly ploughed and sown; and hereon, at a later period, bishop Aldhun erected a tolerably large church of stone … The said bishop, assisted by all the populace, and by Uhtred, earl of the Northumbrians, cut down the whole of the timber, and in a brief space of time made the place habitable. The entire population of the district, which extends from the river Coquet to the Tees, readily and willingly rendered assistance as well to this work as to the erection of the church at a later period; nor did they discontinue their labours until the whole was completed. When the wood had been uprooted, and a residence assigned by lot to each person, the bishop, in the warmth of his love for Christ and St. Cuthbert, commenced to build a fine church upon a large scale, and devoted all his energies to its completion. In the meantime the sacred corpse had been translated from that smaller church … and removed into another which was called the White Church; and there it remained for the three years during which the larger fabric was being built.

It was, then, on 4 September 998, just three years after the community's arrival at Durham, that Aldhun dedicated a large stone church inside which Cuthbert's remains were placed. This building, possibly on the site of the present cloisters, was cruciform in plan and designed to have two towers, one central, another at the west end, both with brass-covered pinnacles. For some reason, the western tower was not finished until many years later but before 1041 while Eadmund was still bishop.

   As time passed, yet more relics were deposited at Durham, drawing even greater numbers of pilgrims. Early in the 11th century, a priest called Elfrid, sacrist to the monastery and sometime guardian of Cuthbert's body, became convinced that it was God's will he should travel around the length and breadth of Northumbria collecting (many, now, would say stealing) the remains of holy people buried there. During his quest he stole the remains of two hermits, two Bishops of Hexham, two abbesses and a king. He even removed the bones of St Boisil from Melrose. There was, however, one set of remains which remained elusive and they were at Jarrow where, it must be supposed, the monks knew of his ways. For several years he was thwarted in his attempts to procure the bones of the Venerable Bede but in about A.D. 1020, after days spent there in prayer and meditation, he left Jarrow never to return. He carried with him the saint's bones which he deposited at Durham. It was not until after Elfrid's death, however, that their precise location was discovered. He had placed them in the coffin with the body of Cuthbert. Nor, yet, was Cuthbert himself to be allowed to rest in peace. The Vikings were no longer a scourge, the great King Canute actually travelling barefoot to Durham to heap honour on him, but close relatives of the Vikings, the Normans, were soon to cause more upheaval for Cuthbert and the Durham monks.

In 1069, just three years after the Battle of Hastings, King William I became concerned when some of the northern earls and Ethelwin, Bishop of Durham, led a rebellion against him. Once it was put down, he created Robert Cumyn, one of his nobles, Earl of Northumberland. When, a short time later, Cumyn and all but one of his soldiers were butchered by the people of Durham, William marched north to exact vengeance.

When Ethelwin and the monks heard of the king's intentions, they took their sacred relics, including Cuthbert's body, and set off by way of Jarrow and Bedlington to Lindisfarne. When, on the fourth day, they stood on the shore opposite the island, they were unable to cross because the tide was in but another Cuthbert miracle intervened. The waters receded, allowing the monks to cross to safety, and covering the way again as soon as the last of the party was over. After four months on Holy Island, they returned the body to Durham but found that William had laid waste the entire countryside between Durham and York, destroying crops, houses and churches as well as slaughtering people indiscriminately. Still, Cuthbert was home again. The mystery surrounding the incorruptibility of Cuthbert's body was to linger on for centuries.

In 1104, when the new Norman cathedral was considered ready to receive the body, which had been resting for some time in a stone tomb in the cloister garth, the decision was taken to inspect the remains again before they were placed in the new tomb behind the high altar. The examination was to be carried out at night by the prior and nine monks, who began their task with all due ceremony on 29 August. Having broken open the coffin lid, they found inside a perfectly preserved oak coffin. They moved the coffin into the middle of the choir and, on opening it, found a linen cloth beneath which lay the body of St Cuthbert looking more asleep than dead. He was lying on his right side. A sweet smell emerged from the coffin, suggesting that the body had been embalmed many centuries earlier. Also in the coffin were various treasures, relics of other saints and, in a small sack, the bones of Bede. The monks found on removing the body that it bent in the middle. Some relics were removed from the coffin into which the body was then replaced, and the whole was moved back into the shrine. It was soon afterwards removed again so that Cuthbert's body could be wrapped in expensive cloth. Many Church dignitaries were present, so important was the moving of the saint's body considered to be, and some of them expressed serious concern about the secretive way in which the monks had just carried out their examination of the body, going so far as to suggest that it was nothing more than a collection of bones or that it was an actor feigning death. Yet another examination was agreed and this time there were about fifty people present. Out came the coffin again. The examiner was a visiting abbot who lifted Cuthbert's head, moved it about and pulled the ears before he was satisfied. The gathering concluded that Cuthbert was dead and that the body was his and had not decayed.

In the 16th century, as part of the Dissolution of the Monasteries, three commissioners of King Henry VIII arrived in Durham to remove the treasures of the cathedral. Suspecting that there might be something of value in Cuthbert's shrine they had it broken open, but the workman charged with the job accidentally broke one of Cuthbert's legs. He saw quite easily that there was a complete body inside, the face sporting a beard. Two of the

19 *St Cuthbert's pectoral cross.*

20 *The silver casing of St Cuthbert's portable altar.*

21   *Detail from the 11th-century St Calais Bible.*

commissioners were called to see this for themselves. They had the body removed to a nearby vestry and waited to hear what the king wanted to have done with it. When nothing was heard from Henry, the bishop had the body reburied behind the high altar beneath a slab of blue marble.

Almost 300 years later, in 1827, several men of influence at the cathedral opened the tomb again. The dean and chapter librarian, James Raine, the man responsible for researching the route of the body's travels in the tenth century, recorded the happenings. The blue marble slab having been removed, the workmen encountered almost two feet of soil beneath which was another stone slab. That having been put to one side, there was revealed a pit some four feet deep, at the bottom of which was a large, but badly decaying oak coffin. Within it was another, in an even worse state of preservation. After a motley collection of human bones had been removed, a third coffin was found, this the most decayed of all. After investigation, the examiners concluded that this was the coffin which had been opened in 1104. Within it was a skeleton, wrapped in five layers of clothes. Secreted deep in this fabric was the wonderful pectoral cross, probably Cuthbert's own, now universally known as a symbol of Durham. This, together with a comb, a portable altar, some clothing and pieces of the original coffin, was removed and displayed first in the dean and chapter library and then in a special room in the cathedral undercroft. The stole and maniple found in the coffin had originally been ordered to be made by Queen Elfleda for the Bishop of Winchester. Two years after this prelate's death, they were brought to Chester-le-Street by King Athelstan as an offering at Cuthbert's shrine. At the end of the examination, all of the human remains were reburied on the site in a new coffin. There was to be yet another opening of the coffin. In 1889 it was confirmed that the skeleton contained in the grave was almost certainly that of Cuthbert. The bones were still covered in a membrane, again suggestive of early embalming. A missing shinbone tallied with the breaking of one of Cuthbert's legs by the workman during the 16th century.

There is a strange legend which surfaces from time to time around the cathedral, a ghost which will not be laid. Soon after Queen Elizabeth I, a Protestant, came to the throne, so the story goes, a small band of Roman Catholic monks broke into Cuthbert's tomb and removed his body. This was then hidden by three of them in another part of the cathedral. When one of the three Benedictine monks died, the other two entrusted a new third man with the secret which has thus been passed down to the present day. Most historians shrug this off as a fairy story, but there are people who believe it. Sir Walter Scott referred to the legend in his *Marmion*:

> There deep in Durham's gothic shade
> His relics are in secret laid,
> But none may know the place
> Save of his holiest servants three,
> Deep sworn to solemn secrecy,
> Who share that wondrous grace.

Even more of a mystery than this legend and the story of the incorruptibility of Cuthbert's body is the comparatively modern find of the pectoral cross. That it is genuine and 'right' is beyond all doubt but in all the investigations of the body and its clothing how was it missed so many times? Perhaps it was, indeed, found on earlier examinations and just quietly replaced in its hiding place. Today it is still safe, one of the greatest treasures not only of Durham Cathedral but of the whole of the Christian world and faith.

Four

DURHAM CATHEDRAL

Durham Cathedral is, by any standards, an architectural masterpiece. It is also a magnificent tribute to those who conceived and built it, knowing full well that they would never witness the complete fruition of their labours but demonstrating their unswerving faith in the future. To these men Durham and the world owe a great debt. The cathedral was not the first building on Durham's peninsula erected to house the remains of St Cuthbert nor is it exactly as its Norman builders first conceived it. Over the centuries there have been some modifications and repairs to the building on which work was started by Bishop William of St Calais in 1092. Compared with its contemporaries, however, Durham has been altered little and remains one of the finest examples of architectural innovation.

From the top of Owengate, the first sight of this awesome and beautiful cathedral is unforgettable, nor does the sensation diminish on subsequent visits. The sheer size of the place, an impression enhanced because it is not, like York for example, surrounded by other buildings, is difficult to absorb. Everything about it is massive but in perfect proportion. The great nave runs for 61 metres and is 12 metres wide, its roof vault rising to some 22 metres. The choir is 40 metres long. The magnificent central tower climbs to a phenomenal 67 metres. The entire building stretches 143 metres from the east wall of the Chapel of the Nine Altars to the west wall of the Galilee Chapel, and its builders really do seem to have been reaching for heaven; the pinnacles of the twin western towers point the way and echo the desire. The work of building this great House of God is ascribed to several distinct periods. Work on the nave, transepts and the four west choir bays took place from 1093 to 1133, and Bishop Hugh Pudsey (du Puiset) added the Galilee Chapel at the west end in 1175; the west towers were built between 1217 and 1226, while between 1242 and 1280 the east end of the choir was altered and the Chapel of the Nine Altars erected. The great central tower was rebuilt between 1465 and 1490.

The first Norman Bishop of Durham, Walcher, wanted to see sweeping changes in the north of England. He was King William's man, from Lorraine, and was determined to stamp William's authority on the church at Durham. The old Saxon cathedral was administered by secular priests who were often indistinguishable from common people. These men married, had children and lived largely as they wished. Bishop Walcher allowed a group of Benedictine monks to come north and to settle in the ruins of the church at Jarrow, his ultimate aim being to oust the Saxon priests from Durham and to replace them with Benedictines. This plan was delayed when he was murdered by a mob at Gateshead in 1080. It was left to his successor, William of St Calais, or St Carileph, to implement the Benedictine move. This he did, having first applied to the Pope for proper permission to set up the new order at Durham. The new, celibate Benedictine monks were installed but the secular monks were not simply evicted. Those who were prepared to embrace the new order were told that they could remain, although only one did so. The rest were dispersed to new homes at Norton, Darlington and St Andrew's Auckland.

It was at this point that Bishop St Calais became involved in a plot against the Conqueror's successor, William Rufus, and when this was discovered in 1088 St Calais retreated to sanctuary in Normandy. While there, he visited some of the new churches being built and when he returned

22 *The east walk of the cathedral cloisters in 1841, engraved by R. W. Billings.*

23 *The central tower of Durham Cathedral.*

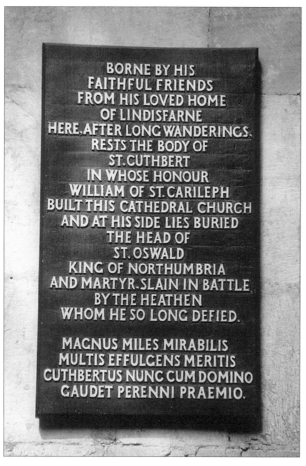

BORNE BY HIS
FAITHFUL FRIENDS
FROM HIS LOVED HOME
OF LINDISFARNE
HERE. AFTER LONG WANDERINGS.
RESTS THE BODY OF
ST. CUTHBERT
IN WHOSE HONOUR
WILLIAM OF ST. CARILEPH
BUILT THIS CATHEDRAL CHURCH
AND AT HIS SIDE LIES BURIED
THE HEAD OF
ST. OSWALD
KING OF NORTHUMBRIA
AND MARTYR. SLAIN IN BATTLE
BY THE HEATHEN
WHOM HE SO LONG DEFIED.

MAGNUS MILES MIRABILIS
MULTIS EFFULGENS MERITIS
CUTHBERTUS NUNC CUM DOMINO
GAUDET PERENNI PRAEMIO.

24 *Explanatory plaque at St Cuthbert's tomb in the cathedral.*

to Durham in 1091, having been given a royal pardon, he was fired with enthusiasm for some of the new architectural ideas he had seen. In 1092 he ordered the demolition of the Saxon cathedral and a year later, on 11 August 1093, the foundation stones for the new monastic church were laid with Malcolm, King of Scotland present at the ceremony. The arrangement St Calais had with the Durham monks was that if they funded the erection of the new monastic buildings he would provide the money for the church which would be built, essentially, with locally quarried sandstone. When he died in 1096, the monks decided that the church should remain their priority and so diverted their finance into that project.

In 1099 Ralph Flambard became the new Bishop of Durham, by which time the nave had been built. Like his predecessor, Flambard also had to flee across the Channel, after escaping from the Tower of London in which he had been incarcerated by the new monarch, Henry I. In Normandy he plotted against Henry and was one of the leaders of an intended invasion of England. After also receiving a royal pardon, he returned to Durham where he continued work on the monastery and church, carrying the walls to the height of the roof. It was during Flambard's episcopate that, on 4 September 1104, St Cuthbert's remains were removed from their temporary cloister home and placed with great ceremony in 'a goodly sepulchre prepared for that purpose' in the new church. In 1593, in the *Rites of Durham*, St Cuthbert's shrine in the feretory, the chapel in which the saint's relics were preserved, is described as being:

... enhanced by an ingeniously made construction of beautiful, costly green marble, and gilded with gold. It was provided with four seats or places below the shrine where pilgrims and others, and especially the sick or lame, might lean or rest as they knelt and made their devout offerings and fervent prayers to God and holy St Cuthbert for his miraculous relief and help. Since such help was never denied, the Shrine was so lavishly invested that it was considered to be one of the richest monuments in England, so many were the offerings and jewelled gifts offered to it.

The cover was made of wainscot and in each corner was fixed a hook of iron from which cords met together over the cover. To these cords was fixed a strong rope which moved up and down through a pulley fixed in the vault above St Cuthbert's Feretory, while the other end of the rope was fixed to the north pillar of the Feretory. Six silver bells were attached to this rope, so that when the cover was raised the lovely sound of the bells drew all the people in the Church to the Shrine to offer their prayers to God and holy St Cuthbert, and to see the marvellous decorations upon it.

Following Flambard's death it was five years before a new bishop was appointed, and between 1128-33 the monks all but finished their church. Bishop Geoffrey Rufus constructed for the monastery a wonderful chapter house.

One of the most powerful of the Durham bishops was Hugh Pudsey (or du Puiset), elected in 1153. Although he did not always get on well with the monks, this was by no means unusual. Pudsey's contribution to the church at Durham was impressive. At first he considered adding to the structure's east end but several accidents hindered progress so significantly that the bishop concluded God did not want changes there. Pudsey looked to the other end of the church and built the Galilee chapel. Before this was created, the main entrance to the church had been through massive western doors, which Pudsey replaced with a new entrance on the north side. Pudsey's architects and builders did not have much space in which to work, there being little land at what was formerly the west end of the church. The chapel is, consequently, very wide, almost 15 metres, in comparison to its length. Built on solid rock, it is felt by many to be the best example in England of transitional Norman/Early English architecture. Although Pudsey was a builder of graceful structures, their foundations were not

25   *Interior of the Galilee Chapel, Durham Cathedral.*

26 *Detail of the fine carving in the Galilee Chapel.*

27 *Inscription beside the tomb of the Venerable Bede, Galilee Chapel.*

always as they should have been and considerable repairs have been necessary through the years. When Thomas Langley became bishop in 1406, the Galilee was in such a poor state of repair that he had a new roof installed and carried out other essential work to prevent the chapel from sliding into the River Wear. He also prevented the future use of the great west doors and created two new entrances to the nave area. Twelfth-century wall paintings are extremely rare in this country but two examples, one believed to be of St Cuthbert, the other of St Oswald, survive here on the north-east side. In the Galilee chapel is the simple tomb of the Venerable Bede. After Bede's bones were moved from Cuthbert's tomb they were placed in a jewelled silver-gilt shrine. The present 'table' tomb, made in 1831 of carboniferous limestone, holds the remains of England's first true historian and the inscription on it reads 'HAC SUNT IN FOSSA BEDAE VENERABILIS OSSA'. Legend tells that the man carving the inscription fell asleep during his task, having intended to chisel '... BEDAE SANCTI OSSA'. When he awoke, he found that the work had been done for him, supposedly by an angel, and a literary one at that!

Richard le Poore became Bishop of Durham in 1228, moving from Salisbury, whose cathedral he had just built. When he first saw the church at Durham, its east end was made up of three semi-circular apses, the central one apsidal inside and out, the two others apsidal within and rectangular outside. They needed urgent attention. Ignoring Pudsey's failure to build there, he conceived the idea of the Chapel of the Nine Altars and chose Richard of Farnham as his architect. As it transpired, the building was not actually started until after le Poore's death when it was erected by the prior, Thomas of Melsonby. Thomas also oversaw the building of the central tower to the height of the gallery, the complete operation taking another quarter of a century.

The great weight of the roof of the Chapel of the Nine Altars is carried on the east wall's external buttresses. The chapel is divided into three bays of unequal size. Before the Reformation there were nine altars against the east wall. From north to south their dedications were to St Michael the Archangel, St Aidan and St Helen, St Peter and St Paul, St Martin, St Cuthbert and St Bede, St Oswald and St Laurence, St Thomas of Canterbury and St Katharine, St John the Baptist and St Margaret, and to St Andrew and St Mary Magdalene. The altars were separated by wooden partitions into which were built cupboards to hold vestments. There was also a wooden canopy over each altar. At the north end of the chapel is a charming memorial to Bishop William van Mildert, founder of Durham University and technically the last of the prince bishops of Durham. Buried just in front of his statue lies the 14th-century Bishop Antony Bek, the first person since Cuthbert to be allowed burial in the cathedral. Just west of Bek's grave is the memorial to the Victorian bishop Joseph Barber Lightfoot, reputed to have been the finest and most able English theologian of his time. Bishop Walter Skirlaw (1388-1405) is buried nearby. In the choir is the tomb of Bishop Thomas Hatfield (1345-81), founder of Durham College, now Trinity

28   *Medieval wall painting of St Cuthbert, Galilee*   **29**   *Sanctuary knocker (replica) on the cathedral*
Chapel.   *north door.*

College, Oxford. It is incorporated within the episcopal throne, 'the highest bishop's throne in Christendom'.

In the very early years of the 15th century, Bishop Walter Skirlaw paid for a great deal of the basic laying out and essential construction work of the monastery cloisters attached to the church. On the west side, the monks' dormitory, 60 metres long and 12 metres wide, was built by him and completed in 1404. Its wooden roof supports are a wonder to behold, 21 enormous oak beams which span the entire width of the room. Beneath the dormitory is the undercroft which used to contain the monks' warming room. The east range of the cloisters contains the chapter house, part of the original early 12th-century building, where the monks would gather to talk through monastic business. It was knocked down at the end of the 18th century but rebuilt in 1895. Beneath the south range is the original Norman undercroft, above which was the refectory, the monks' dining room, converted in 1684 into a library. What is now the cathedral bookshop was originally the 14th-century kitchen with a magnificent stone vaulted roof.

It was in 1429 that Prior John de Wessington, a member of the family from which the American president George Washington was descended, wrote to Bishop Langley giving details of the great storm and resultant fire which had destroyed, overnight, the great central tower of the monastic church. Repairs were put in hand but these were purely temporary. By 1456 the tower was in such a sorry state that the prior informed Bishop Neville of his fears every time there was a storm. Proper repairs were still not begun until 1470 and, even then, only at the lower levels; the upper stage was added between 1484-94. There have been, of course, other minor alterations and repairs to the cathedral over the centuries – and some acts of gross vandalism too.

The main entrance to Durham Cathedral is the great north door which is dated to the mid-12th century. To this was affixed the sanctuary knocker, a criminal's hope of salvation, where fugitives could find temporary shelter and immunity from prosecution even though their pursuers might be at their very heels. It was not, in fact, necessary for the pursued person to grasp the knocker because the boundaries of sanctuary at Durham extended well away from the monastery church, probably as far as Neville's Cross and Gilesgate. The sanctuary knocker on the door today is a replica, placed there in 1980, of the original which is a Romanesque bronze piece 59 centimetres deep and in the form of a lion's head, the mane spread and the eye sockets once possibly having held coloured enamel. There is still uncertainty as to the original knocker's precise age since, while it was probably first placed on the door in the 1150s when Bishop Pudsey created the north porch, it could well have had an earlier home elsewhere on the site.

The English right of sanctuary can be traced back to A.D. 597 when the laws of King Ethelbert of Kent decreed that those who violated the peace of the church would be punished. Later Saxon laws continued the practice, even giving such places as Durham, which was held in high regard because of its Cuthbertian links, special privileges of sanctuary. The Normans continued to observe the tradition. At Durham, sanctuary was granted for 37 days. A fugitive would knock on the door and then be admitted to the church, but only if he were carrying no weapons, by one of the watchers who kept vigil in a small room over the north porch. This room no longer exists. He would then be taken to a grilled alcove where he was given bedding and food. The watcher who had admitted him then tolled the Galilee bell to inform the world outside that a fugitive had been given refuge. The prior was given whatever details were available about the felon. One of the main reasons why Durham was so popular as a place of sanctuary, some runaways travelling there from as far away as Somerset and Surrey, was that it had its own Palatine coroner who could resolve matters quickly. When this official arrived, he heard the man's confession at St Cuthbert's shrine. The fugitive had then to swear an oath promising that he would leave the country as quickly as possible, travelling to a port to seek passage abroad. Should he have failed to find this within 40 days, he had to return to sanctuary. An Act passed during the reign of Henry VIII also required the coroner to witness the branding of the letter 'A' with a hot iron on the flat of the man's right thumb.

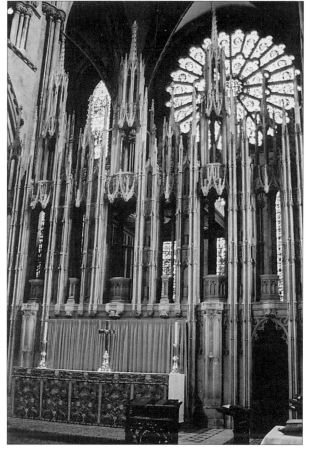

30   *The Neville Screen.*

While in sanctuary, the fugitive was made to wear a black gown with a large yellow cross of St Cuthbert on the left shoulder. He was able to attend services and to wander about the church. Had he the ways and means, he was also allowed to conclude any business he had left unfinished. Towards the end of the allotted 37 days, he was directed to, or chose himself, a port to which he travelled wearing only a single piece of sackcloth clothing and carrying a white wooden cross. The law protected him from being abused as he made his way there. Efforts to end the right of sanctuary, for many and various reasons, were made as early as 1531. Queen Mary attempted to reinstate it but Elizabeth I hastened it on its way and in 1624 the entire system was abolished by King James I.

Durham Cathedral is not cluttered with the multitude of effigies and tombs so often encountered in other great churches. There are tombs and memorials but not in any number and always unobtrusive. One of the reasons for this is that, because of the great sanctity of Cuthbert, not even bishops were initially allowed burial in the church, although this convention was sometimes ignored in later times. A rood screen which used to stand between the two pillars at the east end of the nave was destroyed during the Reformation, along with some 30 altars in various parts of the church, and later vandalism was carried out by thousands of imprisoned Scots.

The carved wooden font canopy, in the area between the north and south doors, dates from 1663 and was probably designed by James Clement, a Durham architect. It is contemporary with the stalls and canopies in the choir, some of which are also ascribed to Clement. It was during the episcopate of John Cosin, that great lover of wood, that so much restoration of the cathedral furniture was undertaken. Just to the east of the font, a line of Frosterley marble set into the floor indicates the point beyond which, under Benedictine rules, no woman was allowed to pass. This was the closest they could approach to St Cuthbert's shrine.

In the nave, a little to the east of the miners' memorial, are the tombs of some members of the once-powerful Neville family of Raby Castle near Staindrop. They had strong connections with the cathedral, were the first lay people to be buried in it and gave money to beautify it. The more easterly tomb is that of the victor of the Battle of Neville's Cross, Ralph, 4th Baron Neville. To the west is the last resting place of his son John, 5th Baron Neville, who in 1372 presented 200 pounds of silver to purchase a new base for St Cuthbert's shrine and 500 marks towards the cost of the Neville Screen, behind the high altar. He was with his father at Neville's Cross. Both men's wives also appear in effigy, Lord John having been married to Maud, daughter of the famed Harry Hotspur. These tombs were later badly damaged by the Scots imprisoned in the cathedral after the Battle of Dunbar. The Neville Screen is a wonderful piece of work. Made in London by Henry Yevele from soft stone, sometimes called Caen stone or Dorsetshire clunch, it was brought by sea, ready-carved and packed in chests, to Newcastle. It was then transported on wagons to Durham and seven masons were engaged for almost a year in erecting it in the chancel. What are now empty niches on this screen were once adorned with 107 statues, probably removed when the monastery was dissolved by Henry VIII. Even without these, the Neville Screen is still an object of great beauty.

The Neville family did not, however, always enjoy the most amicable of relationships with the cathedral. The Raby estate is today renowned for its two fine herds of deer but in the 13th century the Nevilles and the Church actually came to blows over one of these animals. One of the conditions on which the family held

31 *The great clock in the cathedral's south transept, engraved in 1841 by R.W. Billings.*

Raby was that every St Cuthbert's Day they had to present a deer to the abbey at Durham. For a long time this presentation was duly made but in 1290, for some reason, Ralph, 3rd Lord Neville, decided that the time had come to turn the tables on the monks. He declared that he should be entertained by the prior and so should as many of his friends and servants as he chose to bring with him. The prior was astounded by the request and instructed that should a deer indeed be delivered it should not be accepted. The abbey, he protested, could not afford nor be expected to feed so many people. On the appointed day, Ralph Neville and his followers arrived at the north door of the cathedral carrying the stag but, instead of heading for the abbey kitchen, they took the beast, to the accompaniment of blaring hunting horns and much rowdiness, to the Chapel of the Nine Altars. The monks, as instructed, duly refused to accept the offering but Neville simply ordered his men to take it to the kitchen and to cook it themselves. A fight broke out, the monks driving off the Raby men with some large and convenient candles. The argument was taken to litigation, the prior claiming that the routine of the church had been disrupted and Neville countering that he had suffered assault. Although both cases were subsequently allowed to lapse, the 3rd Lord Neville never again delivered the once-required stag.

A list of what was consumed in the abbey at Durham during the course of Whit Week 1346 gives an insight into the diet enjoyed, at least sometimes, by the monks of Durham and their visitors. This was to feed 70 monks and 16 novices as well as guests, helpers and pilgrims:

> 600 salt herrings, 400 white herrings, 30 salted salmon, 12 fresh salmon, 14 ling, 55 kelengs [?], 4 turbot, 2 horse-loads of white fish and a congr [conger eel], playc [plaice], sparling [a type of fish, like smelts], and eels and fresh water fish, 9 carcases of oxen, salted, 1 carcase and a quarter, fresh, a quarter of an ox, fresh, 7 carcases and a half of swine in salt [pork], 6 carcases, fresh, 14 calves, 3 kids [young goats], and 26 sucking porkers, 5 stones of hog's lard, 4 stones of cheese, butter and milk, a pottle [half a gallon] of vinegar, a pottle of honey, 14 pounds of figs and raisins, 13 pounds of almonds, 8 pounds of rice, pepper, saffron, cinnamon and other spices and 1,300 eggs.

A clock in the south transept, which has fascinated visitors for centuries, was set up by Prior Castell, who administered the abbey between 1494 and 1519 and who had made for it a carved oak case. The works and dials were renewed by Dean Hunt in 1632. How it survived the ravages of the Scottish prisoners is a mystery but it was probably useful to them in a purely practical way. It is also said that a thistle carved over the upper dials caused it to be spared. The three dials over the main clock face record the month, the day and the phase of the moon.

A doorway to the west of the clock gives access to the flight of 325 stairs which lead to the top of the great central tower. According to some early sources, the monks watching the Battle of Neville's Cross from there in 1346 began to sing with joy when they knew the Scots had been routed. On the anniversary of the battle each year for a considerable time thereafter a party of monks made its way to the top of the tower and sang three anthems, one to each point of the compass except for the west, where the battle had been fought.

Five

DURHAM CASTLE

Durham City has twin architectural jewels, its magnificent cathedral and, across Palace Green, its ancient and imposing castle. Both survive today as testaments to the highpoints and traumas of a thousand years.

Although the basis of the present castle buildings was begun in 1072 by Waltheof, Earl of Northumberland, by the order of William the Conqueror himself, there were undoubtedly earlier defensive works on and near the present lofty, naturally-defended site. These were used by the Saxon defenders against the unsuccessful siege by the Scottish King Malcolm in 1006 and again, some 30 years later, when the Scots, led on that occasion by King Duncan, were equally frustrated. Unlike the cathedral, Durham Castle does not rest on quite such secure rock foundations and has required a great deal of rebuilding and restoration over the centuries to preserve what is seen today. Although it is now the term-time home of some of the students at Durham's University College, the castle was previously occupied or superintended by successive bishops of Durham, a tenure relinquished only on the death of William van Mildert in 1836.

32 *Durham Castle from South Street.*

47

33   *The keep of Durham Castle from the cathedral tower.*

As the Normans took over England after their victory in 1066 at the Battle of Hastings, they erected a multitude of motte-and-bailey castles across the country. These were, basically, wooden strong-houses, on an artificial mound where no other convenient high ground existed, surrounded by a strong wooden fence and moat or ditch beyond which was another fenced enclosure or bailey. This was the area where people from the surrounding area, along with their animals, could find protection when there was danger of attack and where horses could be stabled and supplies stored.

As time passed, many of these strong-houses were converted into stone castles, their wooden palisades being replaced by more substantial stone walls. Durham had both an inner and an outer bailey and substantial parts of the old bailey walls can still be seen in many of the present Bailey gardens. The outer bailey, especially, is now rather difficult to make out and little remains of the original Norman castle. The stone of that building has obviously been re-used elsewhere on the site but the only original works are the chapel and the undercroft. Of the large hall built on the north side of the courtyard by Bishop Pudsey a century later, there is more substantial evidence but it, too, has been much altered. Another century on, Bishop Bek began construction of what is now the Great Hall on the western side of the courtyard, a huge room added to by Bishop Hatfield in the middle of the 14th century. It was

34 *Interior of the great hall of Durham Castle, 1883.*

35 *The black staircase in Durham Castle, 1883.*

36 *Bishop Cosin's almshouses of 1666 on Palace Green.*

Hatfield, too, who undertook a rebuilding of the keep, at that time part of the original Norman castle. His four-storey creation was erected on an octagonal ground plan. This keep was rebuilt by Anthony Salvin in 1839 to provide accommodation for students at Durham's fledgling university.

Durham Castle has not always been purely a fortress, a bastion against Scottish incursions. Despite its huge proportions, the building has a truly welcoming warmth, a feature which is not accidental. In the early years of the 16th century, the bishops and their retainers seem to have decided that, as there was no longer need for the building to serve as a major fortress, it could be converted into a comfortable lodging. It was then that the shell of the present kitchens was added along with a new chapel. By the time the English Civil War had drawn to a close in the mid-17th century, the castle was gradually taking on a new role. Starting with John Cosin, subsequent bishops used the building for hospitality as well as to demonstrate their great wealth and power.

In its time, the building has welcomed a cavalcade of visitors. Many English monarchs have been entertained here including Edward III, Charles I, James I and all the monarchs of the House of Windsor, including Queen Elizabeth II, as well as a number of Scottish rulers. Accommodation was also provided, until 1971, for Her Majesty's assize judges while they carried out their duties in the city. Hospitality has often been on a lavish scale. When Bishop Cosin was preparing for the arrival of the assize judges in August 1661, the provisions purchased to entertain them included:

> a fat oxe, 9 pigeons, 24 ducks, 16 geese, 36 turkeys, a cage of sturgeon from Darlington, mutton, veal and other butcher meat, ham, neats' tongues, a Holland cheese, sweetmeats wet and dry, oranges and lemons, three loads of malt brewed in the house, three dozen bottles of canary wine, two dozen bottles of sack and a tun of French wine.

The total cost was £140. More than 150 years later, on 3 October 1827, Bishop van Mildert hosted a banquet in the Great Hall in honour of the Duke of Wellington and included among the 50 other male guests Sir Walter Scott.

The courtyard of the castle is an irregular shape and is entered across what used to be a dry moat with drawbridge and via a Norman-cored gateway which was rebuilt by Bishop Flambard in the 12th century and restored again at the close of the 18th century. The massive studded gates were installed by Bishop Tunstall between 1530 and 1559. The keep itself, as seen today, is largely the work of the architect Anthony Salvin who, in 1840, rebuilt the ruins of the 14th-century construction.

The Great Hall was created by Bishop Bek between 1284 and 1311. It was extended in length and had its great timber roof added by Bishop Hatfield 50 years later. Then, at the end of the 15th century, it was reduced to its original size by Bishop Fox who also created the adjoining and magnificent kitchens. Over 30 metres long and 14 metres high, the Great Hall's walls are adorned with arms, banners from the Napoleonic Wars and portraits of the great and famous associated with Durham.

HOSPITALE EPT DUNELM
PRO VIII PAUPERIBUS
FUNDAT PER JOH EPISCOP
A·D·MDCLXVI

37   *Entrance to Bishop Cosin's almshouses, Palace Green.*

38   *Replica Victorian post box, Palace Green.*

Its magnificent timber roof was created on the orders of Bishop Hatfield. The large stained-glass window by Kempe at the north end dates from 1882 when it was created to celebrate Durham University's 50th birthday. At the opposite end of the hall is the modern 'minstrels' gallery'.

Bishop John Cosin's beautiful Black Staircase of 1663 is 17 metres high, climbs four storeys and displays a quite amazing camber as it links Bishop Tunstall's Gallery with the Norman Gallery of Bishop Pudsey. The castle's small Norman chapel, dating from *c.*1080 but with a north wall of even earlier date, was probably unused after the inauguration of Bishop Tunstall's chapel in 1542 until its reintroduction as a place of worship in 1952. Tunstall's Chapel was subsequently enlarged by Bishop Cosin and, in about 1700, by Bishop Crewe.

The large and carefully tended expanse of lawn between castle and cathedral is enclosed on its east and west sides by two beautiful ranges of buildings. This great space was created at the beginning of the 12th century when Bishop Flambard demolished the clutter of houses and the market place which occupied the area between the two then-unfinished Norman buildings. The people who had lived there were probably moved across the river to Crossgate and Framwellgate.

39 *University Library, Palace Green.*

The first building on the left as the Green proper is entered from Owengate was adapted by Anthony Salvin in 1841 from the bishop's coach-house and stables. Set back from it is a modern university accommodation block in keeping with the character and style of the area. Just to the south of it is a modern copy of an acorn-capped Victorian pillar box. The next building on this east side is the brick-built Bishop Cosin's Hall, a late 17th-century three-storey house with a wonderfully elaborate hood to its main entrance. Formerly known as Archdeacon's Inn, it was used as a hall of residence by the university until 1864. The arms of Bishop John Cosin are still to be seen over the main doorway of the stone-built almshouses founded in 1666 and replacing Bishop Langley's dilapidated song and grammar schools of 1414. The almshouses accommodated eight poor people, four men and four women, while the north and south ends of the building were used as schools, one for grammar, the other for plainsong and the art of writing. Next along is the Pemberton Building, looking much older but actually dating only from 1931. On the corner of this range and Dun Cow Lane, once known as Lykegate or Lydgate, the place where coffins were rested, stands Abbey House, built to three storeys early in the 18th century although parts of it are earlier.

At the south end of the buildings to the west of Palace Green is the old grammar school, serving that purpose from 1661 to 1844 and now used by the university. Adjoining it is Divinity House, formerly occupied by the school's headmaster and,

40   *West range of buildings, Palace Green.*

on occasion, by some of the pupils. On a rise in the ground between the old grammar school and the cathedral is a stone cross with a tall, tapered shaft standing on a plinth; it was erected in 1905 to the memory of 'The Officers, N.C.O.s and Men of the Durham Light Infantry who were killed in action or died of wounds or disease in the South African Campaign, 1899 to 1902'. Separating the old school from the other buildings on this side of the Green is Windy Gap, a steep vennel (narrow alley) giving access to the riverbank.

At the other side of Windy Gap are buildings associated with the university library. First, erected in 1822 on the site of the old assize courts of Bishop Cosin, is what was the Diocesan Registry and is now part of the library. A plaque records that a county courthouse stood on this site from 1588 to 1811. The present building was passed to the Union Society in 1935 and then to the library in 1978. Beside it is Anthony Salvin's university library of 1858 with George Pace's 1968 extension, best viewed from the riverbank. Next door is Bishop Cosin's library, built by John Longstaffe at the bishop's expense in 1669, primarily for the use of the clergy of his diocese. Cosin's arms are over the main door. An additional entrance was made in about 1833 as an access to the collection for students of the new university. Finally in this western range of buildings is the Exchequer and Chancery, which used to house the Mint, for some of the bishops coined their own money, and Palatinate Court, erected by Bishop Neville in about 1450. Its ground floor is now below the level of the street. Situated on the cobbles at the north-east corner of the Green, just in front of the wall behind which is the Master's House, there is a small, round, stone plinth affixed to which is a plaque recording the true importance of the area. It reads:

1987. In accord with the principles of the World Heritage Convention, Durham Cathedral and Castle have been designated a World Heritage Site, one of a number of protected areas of outstanding natural and cultural significance in our common heritage. UNESCO.

Six

THE PRINCE BISHOPS OF DURHAM

From the earliest years of the Norman Conquest until the fourth decade of the 19th century, the famous and sometimes infamous Prince Bishops of Durham were essentially the most powerful and influential men in the north of England. They oversaw all the 'business' of Northumbria and were practically monarchs in their own right. They did, indeed, owe and pay allegiance to their sovereign but, because of the geographical position of their domain, that monarch realised full well the essential and crucial role fulfilled by the Bishop of Durham as superintendent of the vast area which was the 'buffer zone' between England and Scotland, two nations which were frequently at, or almost at war with each other.

Many of these men were an amalgam of the religious and the secular because, unlike all other bishops in the land, they had no choice but to be part-churchman, part-soldier, part-politician and all-diplomat, the precise degree of each constituent varying as time and circumstance dictated. They were, in practice, omnipotent beings answerable only to their king. However, before the first Norman Bishop of Durham occupied this exalted position, there was a period of what can best be called a readjustment or refinement of the *status quo*.

Ethelwin (1056-71) was the last Saxon bishop of Durham, with a tenure which extended into the first five years of Norman rule in England. The people of England, and especially those in the North East, did not readily accept their new monarch. Several of the northern earls initially rebelled against William but were later granted pardons after they had sworn allegiance to him. Ethelwin, too, received a pardon for he had espoused the rebel cause. There was still a loud murmur of discontent in Northumbria, however, so William decided to take further measures to reinforce his sovereignty. He created one of his Normans Earl of Northumberland: Robert de Comines (Robert Cumyn) was sent to Durham in 1069 along with seven hundred of the king's best soldiers with dual roles as the earl's bodyguard and enforcers of the king's rule. These troops lived in the city but treated the citizens harshly – so harshly, in fact, that the Durham Saxons tried to resist, for which action several were put to death. Ethelwin had tried to warn the Norman lord that such measures would not help the situation but Comines disregarded the bishop's advice, a decision which was to cost him dear.

When word of the executions spread into the countryside around Durham, the people decided to rid themselves of the tyrant and, although it was February and the depth of winter, large numbers of them travelled to Durham, armed for a fight, and after dark surrounded the city. The Norman troops were living in every part of the city so when dawn came the Saxons broke open the gates of Durham and met no organised resistance. They spread along every street, searching out and killing every Norman they found and arrived, eventually, at the earl's lodging. Having set fire to it, they then killed every Norman who tried to flee the flames. Only one badly wounded soldier escaped the conflagration and the slaughter and fled the city.

King William, when informed of the massacre, travelled north to avenge the deaths of Earl Robert and his men. His vengeance was, as ever, swift and severe and he completely ravaged the entire countryside between York and Durham, leaving not a house nor a crop standing and even destroying several churches. Precisely how many people he put to death is not known but the area itself was reduced to a wasteland. When Bishop Ethelwin heard of the king's march on Durham, he convened a meeting of monks and citizens to decide what should be done to preserve Cuthbert's relics. It was agreed they should be removed to Lindisfarne and that was where they were kept for about four months until the king had withdrawn his troops.

William next began to exercise his authority over the English clergy, ransacking churches in the north with the excuse that he was searching for treasure concealed by those who had rebelled against him. He removed the Archbishop of Canterbury

41 *From left, old Grammar School, 1661 and the former Diocesan Registry, 1822.*

and several other Church leaders from their posts, substituting men of his own choice. Ethelwin tried unsuccessfully to flee abroad and so travelled with men who continued to plot against the king to what they believed to be the safe haven of Ely. The abbot there betrayed the conspirators and Ethelwin was consigned to prison where he died, some say starved to death.

Walcher (1072-80) was the first Norman Bishop of Durham. He was of noble birth and had been educated at Liège. Reportedly a man of the highest principles, he was consecrated at Winchester. Meanwhile, the king, realising the strategic importance of Durham, ordered a castle to be built there. Walcher administered the see of Durham at a difficult time for the Church and the country. Soon after he had taken up the post, Waltheof, Earl of Northumberland, became involved in a plot to remove William from the English throne while he was away visiting his lands in Normandy. Waltheof, it should be stressed, is said to have given nothing but tacit support to the conspirators and yet his conscience soon compelled him to reveal the plot to the Archbishop of Canterbury. As a result, many of those implicated in the matter were executed or mutilated and Waltheof himself was beheaded near Winchester in April 1075. On his death, the earldom of Northumberland was granted or sold by King William to Bishop Walcher who then had enormous power over both the Church and the people of the area. The palatinate powers which then gradually or immediately devolved on the bishop were extensive and complicated. He could levy taxes for the defence and service of the palatinate; he could make truces with enemies; he could raise troops, men between the ages of 16 and 60, to defend his lands; he could impress ships for war. He could hold trials and, when necessary, order executions; he could create barons and order their attendance at his councils. He could mint coins, grant licences to fortify houses, build churches, establish hospitals, give the right to hold fairs and markets and institute corporations by charter. He also held and administered forests and chases. In essence he had royal jurisdiction, civil and military, on both land and sea.

The first bishop to be invested with these powers was not, however, happy with the new situation, nor were the inhabitants of the palatinate. The people were used to their bishop being purely their spiritual leader and they found great difficulty in accepting his new dual role, as, apparently, did the bishop himself. Gradually, Walcher became increasingly unpopular and has been accused of perverting the course of justice for his own ends. He was certainly most unwise in the choice of men he selected to hold important posts in the palatinate. The administration of the earldom of Northumberland was entrusted to Gilbert, one of his relatives, while Leofwin, his chaplain, became archdeacon and ecclesiastical adviser. He is said to have misappropriated many of the church's ornaments and treasures and to have given them to members of his family. Gilbert was an even greater offender against the people, allowing his men to treat them as harshly as they wished.

One of Walcher's friends was a Saxon nobleman called Liulph whose lands also suffered at the hands of Gilbert's men. Liulph and most of his family were murdered in their house and the Northumbrians determined to avenge the deaths, Liulph having been a most popular and highly regarded man. The opportunity for vengeance soon presented itself, the people, rightly or wrongly, blaming Walcher for the misdemeanours of his subordinates. He protested his innocence of any involvement in the murders but his real crime, in the eyes of the people, was that he either failed or refused to bring to justice the real perpetrators.

As part of his civil duties, Walcher had to hold a public assembly of his council and ministers at Gateshead. As soon as he arrived it was obvious that there was going to be trouble, and he had not brought a large bodyguard. The crowd which had gathered was in violent mood and the bishop soon became afraid for his safety. To try to save himself, Walcher offered to bring Leofwin to trial for the murders but the offer came too late. The mob respected neither his authority as Earl of Northumberland nor his sanctity as Bishop of Durham. They surrounded the building

42   *Initial illuminated letter to Ecclesiastes, Du Puiset Bible.*

43   *The prophet Amos, Du Puiset Bible.*

44   *Jonah with three lions, Du Puiset Bible.*

and drew their previously concealed weapons. The bishop fled with some of his retinue into the church. Several of the party were sent outside to try to reason with and even to appease the mob but they were slain. The bishop then ordered Gilbert himself to go out and restore order but his life was brought to a sudden end even as he emerged from the church. Next, the angry crowd set fire to the church. Those still inside the building ran out to escape the flames and smoke but each was killed as he came out. The last out was Walcher himself. A spear brought his life to an end and then the crowd proceeded to hack the body to pieces. Not satisfied with the blood already shed, they next moved to Durham where they laid siege to the castle but, after four days, and having had no success, they returned to their homes. There had to be repercussions and these were soon forthcoming. William sent his brother, Odo, Bishop of Bayeux and Earl of Kent, to avenge the Bishop of Durham's death. He brought with him a large force of soldiers who punished not only the perpetrators of the crime but many innocent people too.

In November 1080, King William nominated as the new Bishop of Durham **William of St Calais** (1081-96) or **St Carileph** as he is sometimes called, abbot of the monastery of St Vincent in Normandy. In 1083 this bishop removed the secular clergy from the church at Durham, replacing them with a fraternity of celibate monks. In 1087 King William I died and was succeeded by William Rufus. William de St Calais was still held in high regard by the new king but he then allied himself with a group of nobles, including Odo, who wanted to replace William Rufus with the Conqueror's eldest son, Robert. The plot came to nothing and in 1091 the Bishop of Durham was restored to his see and gave the church several gold and silver ornaments and a valuable collection of books. He also brought with him plans for a new church at Durham since he considered the Saxon one not magnificent enough to house the remains of St Cuthbert. He therefore had it demolished and, in 1093, laid the foundation stones of a new cathedral.

Then he again fell foul of his monarch and was ordered to appear at court. He tried to excuse himself on the grounds of sickness but the king refused to accept his reasons and demanded that he should present himself at Windsor where, on Christmas Day 1095, he became confined to his bed and died on 6 January 1096. He is recorded as having been an erudite, eloquent and witty genius but one bereft of integrity and fidelity.

Durham was without a bishop for almost four years until the appointment of **Ralph (Ranulph) Flambard** (1099-1128), a man to whom the City of Durham will always owe a huge debt. Not of noble birth, he is said to have bought his nomination to the Durham bishopric for £1,000. He is described as having been a clergyman of ready wit, dissolute morals and insatiable ambition. William II furthered his career and appointed him to several important positions, arguing that he was the only man who, to please a master, was willing to brave the vengeance of the rest of mankind.

Flambard had enemies too and there was an early attempt on his life before he became bishop. While walking one day beside the Thames, he was persuaded to board a boat which was to take him, said its crew, to a meeting with the Bishop of London. Instead, he was transferred to a ship which carried him out to sea where he was to be murdered. His would-be assassins quarrelled amongst themselves and Flambard used bribes and his native wit to have himself put safely ashore.

He had been bishop for just fifteen months when William II was killed in the New Forest. On his death, his younger brother Henry became king and it was not long before, on the advice of his council, he had Flambard committed to the Tower of London. While there, and thanks to the generosity of his friends, the bishop lived in the style to which he was accustomed. Nor was he in the Tower long because in 1101 a rope was smuggled in to him, by means of which he escaped and fled safely to Normandy. There he was protected by Robert, Duke of Normandy, Henry's eldest brother, whom he persuaded to attempt an invasion of England, telling him that the English were far from happy with Henry's new regime. The people would rise up and rally to the duke's cause, said the bishop, and so in July 1101 the duke with Ralph Flambard and a large army embarked on their invasion. As strange as it may seem, after intervention by nobles on both sides, King Henry prevented bloodshed by agreeing to pay back all the money expended by Duke Robert on his expedition. He also granted pardons to those who had helped the duke, restoring to them their estates and privileges.

While Flambard was away from England, King Henry had removed from the see of Durham several of its possessions, including Hexham, Carlisle and Teviotdale. The bishop tried every way he knew to return himself to the king's favour. He levied money from the people of the palatinate and used it to buy expensive gifts for the king and to bribe those around Henry to speak well of his northern bishop. Although he initially failed in his endeavours, the palatinate rights of Durham were gradually restored. As his death approached, Flambard tried to make restitution to the monks and people of Durham for the wrongs he had done them earlier in his life. He had himself carried into the great church where he rested on the altar. There he confessed the injuries he had inflicted and restored to the monks all he had taken away from them. He had already given the church several costly vestments to add to its glory. Finally he ordered that his money was to be given to the poor and all debts owed to him waived – but the king ordered them to be paid to the royal treasury instead.

Five years after Flambard's death, **Geoffrey Rufus** (1133-40), the king's chancellor, was appointed as the next bishop. He had been in office for just over two years when his mentor Henry I died and the bishopric was plunged into a series of troubles arising out of national and international politics. For once, the Bishop of Durham seems to have remained wisely aloof from the power struggle which raged across his lands. During his time, coinage was first produced, with the king's consent, at Durham.

45 *Extract from the 12th-century Du Puiset Bible.*

Throughout the bishop's last illness, his chaplain, William Cumin, was with him for much of the time, primarily out of self-interest. He gained the confidence of several of the bishop's servants and friends, especially the custodians of Durham Castle, and conspired with them to take possession of the castle on the death of Rufus, which he did. Several of the barons supported Cumin's cause and tried unsuccessfully to persuade the monks of Durham to elect him as their new bishop. Cumin even had letters forged endorsing his election to the bishopric, pretending that they had come from the Pope. He strengthened his hold on Durham, preventing messages being sent to or received by the monks and sometimes hindering the arrival of supplies. Some monks had already slipped away to Rome to seek clarification of the situation. They returned with instructions that a new bishop had to be elected within forty days so the monks of Durham chose **William of St Barbara** (1143-52), the Dean of York who, when informed of his new appointment, accepted it rather reluctantly. Eventually, an armed force led by Roger Conyers and barons friendly to St Barbara escorted the new bishop to Durham, hoping that Cumin would abdicate his spurious title, but he would not. St Barbara retreated and continued for 16 months to attempt to take back the bishopric. Finally enthroned at Durham in October 1144, William of St Barbara was an eloquent, dignified and learned cleric.

On the death of St Barbara, both the Prior and Archdeacon of Durham laid claim to the vacant see and it was, therefore, deemed necessary to have a third candidate. The man chosen was then just 25 years old and a nephew of King Stephen. He is best remembered as **Hugh Pudsey** (1153-95) but is also recorded as Hugh Pusaz, Hugh de Puteaco, Hugh de Puiset and Hugh du Puiset. He became one of the most magnificent of Durham's bishops but his rise to power was not based on the surest foundations. It has always been believed that the monks of Durham chose to elect Pudsey because of his noble and wealthy background and because he was young and would, therefore, be pliable. If this was their strategy they made a great mistake, for Pudsey was nobody's puppet. Before being elected to his new post, Hugh Pudsey had been treasurer of York and Archdeacon of Winchester. He was soon engaged in quarrels with the monks of Durham. The prior, Thomas, had the courage to resist the bishop's overbearing manner but the bishop, a greater and more practised politician, undermined his authority and rendered the man's position at Durham so untenable that he left the abbey to go to live on the Farne Islands.

King Stephen died soon after Pudsey was consecrated and the monarch who succeeded him did not hold the prelate in such high esteem. Among Henry II's first acts was the reclaiming of Northumberland and Cumberland from Scotland. For a time, an uneasy peace existed between the two kingdoms, apart from some mutual border skirmishing. When William the Lion came to the Scottish throne he decided to take up the cause of one of Henry's rebellious sons, and in 1173 he led a large army across the border and was given free and safe passage through the palatinate by Bishop Pudsey, who soon became one of the prime movers of a truce when an English army advanced to halt the Scottish invasion.

The Scots retreated for a while but then returned with an army of 80,000 men to ravage several northern castles. When an English army marched to meet them, the Scots again retreated, this time to Alnwick, and William was taken prisoner. On the same day, a force of 40 Flemish knights and 500 infantry under the command of Pudsey's nephew landed at the port of Hartlepool. In the light of King William's capture, however, Pudsey immediately sent the foot-soldiers back to the continent while retaining the horsemen and his nephew to garrison the castle he had rebuilt near Northallerton. The Flemish troops were possibly part of a plot by one or more of King Henry's sons to usurp his throne. When William the Lion was eventually brought before the King of England, Hugh Pudsey was ordered to appear too for, of all the English bishops, only he had given Henry cause to doubt his loyalty when he had allowed the Scottish army to march unhindered across his lands and let the Flemish troops land at one of his ports.

There was comparative harmony between England and Scotland for the rest of Henry's reign and in 1188 he agreed to go with the King of France on a crusade. To finance the venture, Henry levied a tax and one of those appointed to collect the money was Hugh Pudsey. Before the king could embark on his crusade, he died in France and was succeeded by his son, Richard the Lionheart, who made his own preparations for a crusade. At the time, many English churchmen were fired with the new king's zeal for a crusade and the Bishop of Durham was not excluded. He, too, levied money for the enterprise and used it to build a galley to carry him on the expedition and to construct other ships for his extensive retinue. This Bishop of Durham was not one to be eclipsed by his peers. He wanted to display greater finery than any of the other bishops and abbots and went to great lengths to outshine them, but Pudsey was destined never to embark on the great crusade.

King Richard preferred the bishop to stay in England, having greater need of the money and vessels he had assembled than of his services abroad, but he had to convince Pudsey to remain at home. He knew that to do so he must appeal to his bishop's vanity, so he asked him to be one of two regents who would look after the realm in their monarch's absence. No sooner had the bishop agreed than the king asked him for a loan of the money and goods he had assembled for the crusade. The bishop was not prepared to part with these without having something more permanent than a regency in return so he persuaded the king to create him Earl of Northumberland for the duration of his life and to confer on him and all future bishops of Durham the earldom of Sadberge, along with its lands. As earls of Sadberge, the bishops of Durham were entitled to add to their mitre an earl's coronet and to display the sword along with their pastoral staff. This may have been when the concept of the Prince Bishops first began. Before the king left on the crusade, Pudsey also paid him £1,000 to be appointed Chief Judiciary of all England and Governor of the castle and forest of Windsor.

46 *Seal of Bishop Hugh Pudsey.*

When Richard was making his way back from the crusade, he fell foul of Duke Leopold of Austria whom he had once affronted and who handed him over as a prisoner to the Emperor Henry VI. When a ransom was demanded for the king's release the Bishop of Durham was one of those who levied funds to furnish the money to free him, but when the king returned to England he appeared to be displeased with Pudsey, who could not understand why. In an attempt to clear the air, the bishop resigned to him the earldom of Northumberland. The trouble, however, lay elsewhere. The king had learned of the large sums of money which had been raised for his ransom by the prelate, only a small proportion of which had actually been used for its intended purpose. Nor had the bishop tried to conceal his great wealth, building a church at Darlington and carrying out other costly projects, so the king decided to fine him. When the bishop offered Richard a large sum of money if he would restore his former honours, the king agreed but insisted that Pudsey should travel to London to deliver the inducement in person. Pudsey set off on his journey. Stopping to rest at Crayke, to the north of York, he apparently dined too well and became ill. He managed to continue his journey as far as Doncaster but was then unable to ride any further and died, aged seventy.

In about 1180, Pudsey had granted a charter for the founding of a priory at Finchale, about four miles from Durham on land which had been given to the monks by Bishop Flambard. One of the most feared diseases of Pudsey's time was leprosy and so he built, at Sherburn, a hospital for 65 lepers, endowing

47   *The cathedral south door, looking into the cloisters, engraved by R.W. Billings.*

it and providing a master and chaplains for the patients. He also had a hospital built at Witton Gilbert, just to the west of Durham City, and another, which he also endowed, near Northallerton. He constructed Elvet Bridge across the River Wear at Durham, built more of the city wall and ordered the reconstruction of the village of Elvet which had been burned to the ground when Cumin usurped the see. One of Pudsey's greatest achievements was the compiling of a record for which historians owe him a great debt. Durham had not been included in William I's Domesday Book of 1086 so the bishop's survey of 1183, known as the Boldon Buke, provided a vast amount of information about the palatinate as it was in the late 12th century.

History has categorised Pudsey's successor **Philip of Poitou** (1197-1208) as a thoroughly bad man. He accused the convent of trying to usurp his authority by attempting to exercise powers which had never before been theirs. The arguments increased in intensity until the bishop decided to settle the matter by ordering his

48 *Detail of Christ in Judgement from a 15th-century cope, re-made in the 17th century.*

troops to besiege the great church. He had them attack the doors and windows with fire and smoke, stopped food reaching the monks and made sure that they had no access to grain from their mill. He destroyed their fisheries, cut off part of their water supply and slaughtered their cattle. When de Poitou was refused admission to the chapter house, he excommunicated the entire chapter and the prior and interrupted one of their services on the festival of St Cuthbert. Accompanied by a riotous mob, he stormed into the church, caused general havoc and manhandled the monks and the prior. The bishop was, it must be said, loyal to King John and supported him through his quarrels with the Pope. For this, de Poitou was excommunicated and died in that state. He could not be interred with the usual pomp and had to be buried in unconsecrated ground.

Richard Marsh, or **de Marisco** (1217-26), initially got along quite well with the monks and confirmed their 'liberties and privileges', even giving them the churches of Dalton, Ayclffe and Pittington, but the truce was destined not to last. It was not long before the monks were accusing their bishop of what amounted to a catalogue of crimes. Bishop Marsh was extravagant, they told the Pope, condemning him also for bloodshed, simony (selling ecclesiastical preferment), adultery, sacrilege, rapine (plundering), perjury (giving false evidence) and of allowing Church property to fall into disrepair. Marsh, however, circumvented justice by, it is said, bribing the papal authorities to protract the case. He was not so easily able to escape the English courts and was forced to travel to London with an entourage of lawyers to answer some of the accusations. One of the breaks in this long journey was at the monastery at Peterborough where the next morning he was found dead in his bed. Foul play was suspected because, before retiring that night, he had been perfectly healthy.

Richard le Poore (1228-37) came to Durham with a good reputation, having done well in his previous incumbencies of Chichester and Salisbury. There he had demonstrated himself to be wise and charitable and he was definitely a great improvement on his two predecessors at Durham. He was on very good terms with the monks and went to a great deal of trouble to set down legal procedures to obviate future arguments between bishop and convent. The agreement was known as Le

49 *Detail of the Crucifixion, from a 15th-century cope.*

50 *Detail of Christ carrying the Cross, from a 15th-century cope.*

Convenit and, by it, Richard gave up for himself and his successors all rights to the title and privileges of Abbot of Durham. In future, he decreed, the prior would rule the convent and there would no longer be any valid reason for the bishop to interfere in the internal affairs of the monastery. He did, nevertheless, retain his nominal title as head of the convent and the prior was never referred to as the abbot.

The next bishop, **Nicholas of Farnham** (1241-49), was an educated man who had studied pharmacy, logic and natural philosophy before turning his attention to theology. He was, apparently, reluctant at first to accept the bishopric of Durham, a rich living, having some time earlier rejected the see of Coventry, a much poorer prospect. It needed the intervention of the Bishop of Lincoln to persuade Farnham that it was his duty to accept the vacancy at Durham in case the king should appoint instead an inferior person. As events transpired, Nicholas was not long in post but he did not die as Bishop of Durham. Instead, he resigned the see in 1249 and went into retirement, having enough money assigned to him for his support. Much of his later life was spent at Stockton-on-Tees where he died in 1257.

In 1255, Bishop **Walter of Kirkham** (1249-60) excommunicated and imprisoned several of the servants of the powerful John Balliol who had forcibly entered Long Newton church. In retaliation, Balliol arranged for the bishop to be ambushed and quite severely beaten, after which he imprisoned four of Kirkham's servants in Barnard Castle. The king ordered their release, regarding the whole matter as an insult to the Crown. The bishop's men were set free but he refused to give up the excommunicants until ordered by law to do so. Balliol College, Oxford, was later founded by the offending baron's widow, this being the penance exacted by Kirkham.

Robert of Stichill (1261-74) as a young man was a monk at Durham and was bishop during one of the most troubled periods of English history.

Robert de Insula (1274-83) was described as a simple, jolly monk of humble origin who, before his election as bishop, had been Prior of Finchale. He was consecrated bishop by Walter Giffard, Archbishop of York. Both men were soon afterwards ordered to send a considerable amount of financial assistance to aid King Edward I in his campaign against the Welsh. In 1276 de Insula held a synod to consider the payment of tithes and other dues, something which was causing problems at the time

Anthony Bek (1283-1311) was another of the 'giant' bishops of Durham. Able, ambitious, fearless, quarrelsome, cold, splendid, dangerous and calculating, he was a statesman. Before becoming bishop, he had been secretary to the king, Archdeacon of Durham and holder of five other livings. He was held in high regard as a negotiator. Before the Scottish war, he was sent to Germany to arrange an alliance against France between the English monarch and the German emperor, and in 1295 he met two cardinals sent by the Pope to try to reconcile King Edward and the King of France. On this latter occasion he showed a fine command of the French language.

He supported his king with more than just advice and prayers during the campaigns against Scotland. In one of these he personally led a wing of the army and did so in grand style. With him went 26 standard-bearers of his household and his train was made up of 140 knights. A thousand infantrymen and 500 cavalry marched under the banner of St Cuthbert, the banner itself being carried by a monk from Durham. The bishop was even wounded in one skirmish and led a section of the English army, with 39 banners at its head, into the Battle of Falkirk, an engagement which decided the success of Edward's campaign. Fifteen thousand Scots are said to have been slain at Falkirk but Bek had angered some of his own Durham people by forcing them to march north of the River Tyne even though they had long enjoyed the 'Haliwerfolc' privilege which insisted that, in doing military service, they were not required to cross the Tyne in the north nor the Tees to the south.

Bek also interfered in the affairs of the convent and relations between him and the prior became strained. The bishop evicted the prior, invaded his park at Bearpark just outside Durham, slaughtered the game there and then laid siege to the convent.

At the time of this dispute, the king was journeying towards Carlisle and called at Durham to help resolve the matter. He ordered the restoration of the prior and warned that the first of the two men to lapse into the quarrel again would become his enemy. It was not long before Bek broke the uneasy truce and set about replacing Prior Hotoun with the Prior of Holy Island. Hotoun was forcibly pulled from his chair by the bishop's men and Prior Luceby installed in his stead.

If the king needed excuses to strike back at the bishop, he now had them in plenty. Bek angered him further by admitting that he sided with those nobles who were then daring to challenge some of the king's privileges. It was a move for which the king never forgave him. Next, Bek left England without the king's permission. He had failed once before to obey a summons to attend the Pope in Rome and, having received a second, decided this was an expedient time to journey to Italy. Believing it was better to be on the offensive than to try to defend his position, he ensured that his entry into Rome was a magnificent spectacle. Despite Bek adopting a rather offhand manner with the Pope, the two men got on well and the bishop was granted the right to visit the convent at Durham, with a small retinue, as and when he pleased.

During Bek's unsanctioned absence from England, the king deprived him of his see and replaced him with custodians. It was not until the next year that his lands were returned to him. In 1306 the bishop was again deprived of his bishopric for what were seen as further abuses of his position but this time the King went further than he had gone before. He severed Barnard Castle from the palatinate and also took away the port of Hartlepool along with Wark in Tynedale, Penrith in Cumberland and Simonburn in Northumberland. King Edward I was succeeded by his son, Edward II, and Bek obviously ingratiated himself with the new monarch who restored the bishop's privileges and created him Lord of the Isle of Man. The Pope had already made him Patriarch of Jerusalem, so he held, at the last, a formidable array of titles.

Bishop Bek, the Prince of the Prince Bishops as he has been called, died at Eltham, near London, in March 1311. He was buried in the east transept of the cathedral at Durham, the first bishop to be interred in the great church. One of the best stories about him concerns a very expensive roll of beautiful cloth which someone foolishly described as being too expensive even for the Bishop of Durham. Bek is said to have been so incensed that he bought the entire roll and then used it as covers for his horses.

Richard of Kellawe (1311-16) is remembered for his high morals, as a man of letters and as a person who was both dignified and eloquent. From the start, the relationship between him and the monks of Durham was harmonious and, far from keeping them at a distance, as had been the custom of so many of his predecessors, Kellawe gave several of them senior positions around him, enjoying their company and that of the convent in general.

51   *Detail of the Resurrection, from a 15th-century cope.*

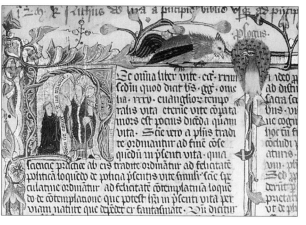

52   *St Cuthbert with the head of St Oswald, from a 14th-century manuscript.*

53   *Seal of Bishop Hatfield, 1345-81.*

Edward II was still having trouble with the Scots who, under Bruce, continued to harry the north of England so vigorously that he asked the Pope to excuse Kellawe from attending the Council of Vienna; he was so desperately needed to defend England's northern border. In 1314 Bishop Kellawe provided the king with a thousand Durham men and one thousand marks for the campaign against the Scots which resulted in the humiliating English defeat at the Battle of Bannockburn. Earlier, following an incident during which the Scots had burned part of the outskirts of Durham, Kellawe had paid them one thousand marks to leave the rest of the city untouched and, on their future marches south, to travel straight through his lands without causing any damage. They did not, of course, comply with the agreement and the bishop was subsequently instructed never again to enter into such a pact.

Lewis Beaumont (1318-33) was the man regarded by many as having been the worst Bishop of Durham of all. He has been described as a disagreeable, ignorant, mincing popinjay who even had the greatest of difficulty with his Latin. As he was travelling to Durham following his appointment, accompanied by two visiting papal cardinals, his party was waylaid at Rushyford, just to the south of Ferryhill, by an armed band led by Gilbert of Middleton, keeper of Mitford Castle near Morpeth. Middleton actually had no grievance against the new bishop – his quarrel was with King Edward – but this ambush was one way he saw of hitting out at the monarch. Consequently, the bishop and his brother, Lord Henry Beaumont, were carried off as prisoners to Mitford Castle where they were held to ransom. The two cardinals were merely robbed and sent to Durham to explain what had happened. To raise the money demanded for the bishop's liberty, the Prior of Durham had to sell off many of the convent's treasures. The ransom was eventually paid and Beaumont was consecrated at Westminster in March 1318.

The Scottish incursions into northern England continued and, as if they were not trouble enough, Beaumont's relationship with the Durham monks, which had not been good from the outset, deteriorated. He had once said to them, 'Do nothing for me as I do nothing for you. Pray for my death, for whilst I live you shall have no favour from me.' He obviously repented to a degree for he did, eventually, give the monks half of his annual income from the village of Edmundbyers.

Richard Bury (1333-45) was a great literary bishop, a lover of books and friend of Petrarch. After leaving grammar school, he attended Oxford University before moving north to Durham to become a Benedictine monk. From there, he was selected as a tutor to the prince who was to become King Edward III. Subsequently he was appointed High Chancellor and then Treasurer of England. Not only was Bury a learned man; he was also a great philanthropist. He surrounded himself with some of the cleverest rising churchmen of his day, men who would go on to become bishops and archbishops in their own right. Bury's greatest act of generosity, however, and that for which he is best remembered today, was his founding of England's first lending library, not at Durham but at Oxford. It was to be used by the students of Durham, later Trinity College. He also wrote a book, *Philobiblion*, which contained instructions for the administration of the library, for the preservation of the books and the conditions on which those books were to be loaned. King Edward III also facilitated Bury's entry into many monasteries where he was able to unearth volumes which had lain hidden and unread for centuries.

Thomas Hatfield (1346-81), the next Bishop of Durham, was secretary to the king and Keeper of the Privy Seal. Soon after his consecration, the Scots, led by Sir William Douglas, again invaded England, burning Carlisle and Penrith before being forced back across the border. Hatfield was overlord of the palatinate at the time of the greatest medieval battle immediately outside Durham City. The incidents leading to the Battle of Neville's Cross were linked directly to the aftermath of the famous Battle of Crécy in 1346, following which the English king moved on to besiege Calais. The French king, who was an ally of the Scots, sent both money and men to Scotland to help finance another invasion of England while Edward was still in

France. Edward, in return, sent commissioners to King David II of Scotland offering to return Berwick to Scotland if he would leave England alone, but David would have none of it. He knew that Edward had taken England's best fighting men with him to France and that the country had rarely been so vulnerable, so assembled a huge army and marched into England, coming eventually to the Beaurepaire (Bearpark/Redhills) area just outside Durham City, expecting an easy passage south. Many of the English nobles and bishops who were not in France had, however, assembled an army and marched to defend Durham:

On 16 October, 1346, the English forces lay in Auckland park. The next day they moved forward, and, after gaining the rising grounds, halted at Merrington, from whence the motions of the Scots on the western hills might be plainly distinguished. The English leaders hesitated whether to advance or to observe the enemy, and expect his attack in so favourable a position. The marshals and standard bearers moving a little forward, the troops insensibly followed them, and thus they proceeded slowly to Ferryhill. Here a strong foraging party of the Scots, under Douglas, fell unexpectedly into the midst of the English troops and were pursued with the loss of 500 men as far as Sunderland bridge. The English halted again on the high grounds above the Wear, but the standard bearers went forward, and the army moved slowly on in order of battle, leaving Durham on the right, to the moor near Neville's cross. Douglas, who had escaped from the slaughter of his pursuers, meanwhile reached the Scottish camp, and gave the first information of the approach of the English force. David had employed the preceding day in drawing out his troops on Durham moor, in order of battle, with standards flying, and had passed the night in Beaurepaire park and wood, without the precaution of a scout or sentinel on the watch. The prudent advice of Douglas to retreat to the hills and avoid an engagement was rejected with disdain and, the Scots advancing to meet the attack, the armies joined battle on the Red-hills, a piece of broken and irregular ground rising swiftly from the Wear. The Scots were formed in three divisions, under the king, the earl of Murray with Sir William Douglas and the high steward of Scotland. The English distributed their force in four bodies. Lord Percy led the first, Lord Neville the second, Sir Thomas Rokeby, sheriff of Yorkshire, commanded the third, and a strong body of cavalry under Edward Baliol, formed the reserve. On a little hillock in the depth of Shawwood, called the Maiden's Bower, the prior with his attendants knelt around the holy corporax cloth of St. Cuthbert, which in obedience to a miraculous vision, was elevated on the point of a spear within sight of both armies. The city of Durham lay in dreadful suspense, a prize to the conqueror; and whilst the remaining brethren of the convent, poured forth their hymns and prayers from the highest towers of the cathedral, their eyes wandered with anxious doubt over the field of approaching combat. The Scots were severely galled as they advanced by the English archers and John Graham, impatient at seeing his men fall without the means of resistance requested of the king an hundred lancers to break the archers. His request was denied and the troops were ordered to keep the line of battle. Actuated at once by courage and indignation, Graham threw himself singly or with few attendants amongst the archers, dispersed them on every side and fought till his horse was struck by a broad arrow and, himself wounded and bleeding, was scarcely able to regain the ranks of his countrymen with life. The high steward immediately led his division to the charge with broad swords and battle axes. The archers were driven back through Lord Percy's division which they disordered in their retreat and the Scots, pursuing their advantage, threw the whole of the body into confusion. Victory hovered on the side of the invaders but the day was restored by the courage and decision of Edward Baliol. With a powerful body of cavalry, he made an impetuous charge on the high steward's divisions and drove them from the field. King David was meanwhile engaged with equal fortunes against Lord Neville and Baliol, suffering the high steward to retreat unmolested, threw himself on the flank of the royal troops which was left uncovered by his flight. The disorder of the Scots became irretrievable and their third body, under the earl of Murray, were cut to pieces amongst the inclosures which prevented their escape. After all was lost, a gallant band of nobles formed themselves around their king, and fought

54   *The cathedral cloisters – the north and east (part) ranges.*

with the courage of despair till only eight of their number survived. David, after receiving two arrow wounds and resisting several attempts to take him captive, was compelled to surrender to John Copeland, a Northumbrian esquire, two of whose teeth he dashed out with his clenched steel gauntlet. Besides the king, the earls of Fife and Monteith and Sir William Douglas, were made prisoners. The earls of Murray and Strathmore, John and Alan Steward, and a long list of Scottish nobility were amongst the slain. Of the English leaders, Lord Hastings alone fell. Copeland was rewarded by the English king with £500 a year in land, and made a knight banneret. Out of an army of 30,000 Scots and French auxiliaries, 15,000 were left dead upon the field whilst the loss of the English was very trifling. (M.A. Richardson, *Local Historian's Table Book,* 1846)

Lord Ralph Neville, one of the heroes of the Battle of Neville's Cross, died in 1347 and became the first layman to be buried in Durham Cathedral.

After the surrender of Calais, there was a truce between England and France but, although Scotland was included in the temporary peace, a great many Scottish raids continued along the border. Hatfield was one of the bishops who was a good friend to the convent at Durham, giving it land at Henknowle, near St Andrew's Auckland, to sustain a priest. In London, he built a palace in the Strand and helped Oxford's Durham College, greatly supplementing its endowment. To the convent he bequeathed various of his personal treasures, one of which was a thorn given to him by Edward III and said to have been from the crown of thorns worn by Christ during his passion.

John Fordham (1381-88), secretary to the king and prebendary of York and Lincoln, succeeded Hatfield and is judged to have been one of the worst of the Durham bishops. He was once described as 'a traitor, a flatterer, a whisperer, a slanderer and a wicked person'. When the English nobles grew tired of Richard II's shortcomings as a monarch, they marched on London to demand that he remove his favourites from office. Included among these was John Fordham. The barons had determined that the bishopric should have a more worthy incumbent and so he was removed from the episcopal throne and exiled to retirement in Ely where he died in 1425.

Before coming to Durham, **Walter Skirlaw** (1388-1405) had been Bishop of Lichfield and Coventry and then of Bath and Wells. He was another of the great builder-bishops of Durham. Eschewing the great affairs of state, Skirlaw was a man with a mission to build and with a desire to bury the memory of his immediate predecessor.

Thomas Langley (1406-37) was Lord Chancellor of England. He is regarded as the last of the great medieval prince bishops. In 1411 he was one of the commissioners on the Scottish border and he also received his cardinal's hat from Pope John XXIII. He was subsequently sent as ambassador to France at a time when both nations were tired of fighting each other. It was he who completed the building of the cloisters and who put in place the repairs so necessary to stop the cathedral's Galilee Chapel from slipping into the River Wear. On Palace Green he built two schools, and ordered the construction of an enormous gateway to Durham Castle.

Little more than a century after Langley's death, as part of Henry VIII's dissolution of the monasteries, the convent at Durham ceased to exist but the buildings themselves, created or watched over by so many of Durham's bishops, survived – spared the ignoble fate of so many other monastic houses which were sold off and in many cases destroyed.

Seven

THE MEDIEVAL TOWN

During the early Middle Ages, Durham's peninsula was and needed to be a fortress, a compact military and religious domain ruled over by successive bishops and priors, peopled by monks and soldiers. Outside its well guarded, substantial walls, but under its military and ecclesiastical umbrella lay the homes, churches and workplaces of the 'common people', as did the pivotal market place, created by Bishop Flambard early in the 12th century to replace that which used to exist in the space which is now Palace Green, where goods, produce and services were traded. This move was strategically sound since it denied free access into the heart of the city's defences. The town walls were added to the fortifications in the 14th century.

Durham, outside the fortified peninsula, consisted of the Barony of Elvet and four other boroughs, the Old, the Bishop's, Elvet and St Giles. Each of these

55 *Elvet Bridge, looking towards Old Elvet.*

73

56 *Morris dancers in the market place.*

settlements, while being recognisably a constituent part of the greater whole, had its own identity, church and public services. Important to urban development and to the rapid growth of commerce, since fording places across the River Wear could be rendered useless during periods of heavy rain, were Durham's great stone bridges. Elvet Bridge, originally built by Bishop Hugh Pudsey in about 1160 and altered in 1228, had more work carried out on it in 1495 by Bishop Richard Fox but it was not until 1804, after much of it had been destroyed in the great floods of 1771, that its original width was doubled. There used to be a chapel at each end, that on the east built late in the 12th century and dedicated to St Andrew while at the west end was a chapel to St James. The earlier Framwellgate Bridge, of about 1120, had been built by Bishop Ralph Flambard who also strengthened the river banks in that area below the castle. When destroyed by flooding at the start of the 15th century, the bridge was rebuilt by Bishop Langley. It was widened in 1828.

St Oswald's church, Durham's oldest, across the Wear gorge to the south-east of the cathedral, met the spiritual needs of the residents of both the borough and the barony of Elvet. Dedicated to the Northumbrian Christian monarch who died in battle at Maserfield near Oswestry, Shropshire in A.D. 642, the date of the foundation of this church is difficult to establish, the oldest parts of the present building being late 12th-century. By 1834, land subsidence and general neglect of the site necessitated the first of several renovations, this one undertaken by Ignatius Bonomi. Further work was carried out 30 years later when 24 medieval grave covers were used to repair the tower stairs and Hodgson Fowler added the vestry to the chancel. Several pieces of Anglo-Saxon stone-work have been found on this site, fuelling the theory that there was an earlier church here. After the great and tragic fire in 1984 there was a chance for arch-aeologists to discover what type of church had previously occupied this site. In A.D. 762 Peohtwine was consecrated Bishop of Galloway somewhere in Elvet, and 15th- and 16th-century maps of the area appear to show that the church had a circular, Saxon-type graveyard. What the archaeologists found was that there had been an earlier church on the site with a typically Saxon apsidal or semi-circular east end.

57 *Remains of 14th-century Kepier Hospital, photographed c.1880.*

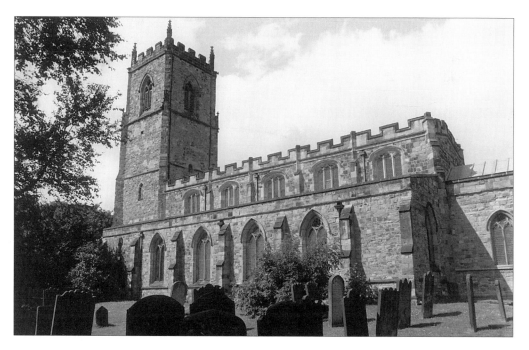

58 *St Oswald's church.*

59 *Remains of the 15th-century Chapel of St Mary Magdalene, Gilesgate.*

The church of St Giles, built by Bishop Flambard on Gilesgate and dedicated by him on St Barbara's Day, 11 June 1112, was the chapel created to serve the hospital of St Giles which was destroyed by fire in 1144 during the illegal attempt by William Cumin to take over the bishopric. It rose from its ashes but on a new site beside the River Wear when it was rebuilt by Bishop Pudsey some ten years later at Kepier, to the north. A master and 13 brothers, six of them chaplains, saw to the needs of visiting pilgrims and others, including in 1298 the king, Edward I. Today little more than a 14th-century archway remains to hint at its former grandeur. A ruin is all that remains, too, of the tiny chapel of St Mary Magdalene, built in 1451 at the bottom of Gilesgate, between St Giles' church and Kepier, an object of curiosity beside the busy road from Durham to the east.

St Nicholas is the patron saint of merchants so it is perfectly appropriate that the church in the market place is dedicated to him. The present lofty Victorian building of 1857 replaced, on the same or a very similar floor plan, the dilapidated and frequently patched medieval 'town' church built by Bishop Flambard before 1128 and described in 1787 as 'very plain and meanly built, being constructed of small and perishable stones, so that from frequent pointing it is now almost covered in mortar'. The old building, with its tower, had undergone extensive, often makeshift, repairs over the centuries and had even suffered the ignominy of being almost hidden from view by a nine-arched piazza built in 1780 in front of almost the whole of its south face. In 1841 its east end had been shortened so that Claypath, one of the roads into

60   *Claypath in the late 19th century.*

the market place, could be widened. The nearby Clayport Gate, part of the city's medieval defences, had been demolished on similar grounds in 1791.

Between St Nicholas' church and the Town Hall is an alley whose position once saved the life of an arrogant archbishop. In 1283, just a few weeks after the death of Bishop Robert de Insula, Archbishop Wickwane of York travelled to Durham to claim, not for the first time, that he had 'rights of visitation' there. He was refused admission to the cathedral and so made his way down to the market place and the church of St Nicholas. Gaining entrance, he climbed into the pulpit and began to excommunicate the Durham monks. On hearing of the archbishop's presence in the city and the reasons for it, a band of angry citizens gathered at the church. So afraid was Wickwane that he fled in terror, but the mob had not been idle while they hastened his departure and had cut off one of his horse's ears. The prelate's life was saved only by the intervention of one of the king's commissioners who was present, who diverted the attention of the angry crowd while Wickwane sped off along Walkergate to the comparative safety of nearby Kepier Hospital. Walkergate is a street name which indicates a connection with the medieval guilds: 'walkers' were fullers or cloth merchants.

Close to the church stood a house called New Place, referred to locally at the time as the Bull's Head, built during the Middle Ages as a palace for the powerful Nevilles of Raby and Brancepeth, the Earls of Westmorland. In its prime, this was an extensive property extending some way up Claypath and with gardens running down to the river. After his unwise involvement in the plot against Queen Elizabeth I, the Rising of the North of 1569, planned at Raby Castle and Brancepeth, the earl forfeited this and other of his property to the Crown. It was eventually bought from King James I in 1612 by Henry Smith's Charity and used as a woollen factory, a workhouse and a charity school before it was demolished, the last evidence of it disappearing in 1853. The charity school was the Blue Coat School, founded in 1708. It initially taught just six boys but by 1732 had 50 pupils, 20 of them girls. In 1812 the school moved to a new site on Claypath.

Also near St Nicholas' church, on the west side of the Market Place, are Durham City's main civic buildings. The medieval Guildhall, of 1356, dates from the time of King Edward III. In 1535 Bishop Tunstall caused it to be considerably rebuilt before giving it to the city. Further rebuilding was undertaken by Bishop Cosin in 1665 and other major alterations were made in 1752. Many of the coats of arms for the old city guilds can still be seen there. Medieval in origin, the guilds were jealous guardians of their privileges. Their main functions were to oversee and guarantee the maintenance of high standards of workmanship in their craft and to ensure, as far as possible, a monopoly of work for their members. They also supervised carefully the admission of new apprentices to the craft, monitoring their long progress to full membership. Sometimes the guilds undertook the provision of pensions for elderly or infirm members and assisted with funeral arrangements. Between the years 1450 and 1667, although some were established much earlier, the craft and merchant guilds of the City of Durham, with the dates when they were established or first recorded, included:

Weavers and Websters, 1450; Cordwainers, 1458; Barber surgeons, Waxmakers, Ropers and Stringers, 1468; Skinners and Glovers, 1507; Butchers, 1520; Goldsmiths, Plumbers, Pewterers, Potters, Painters, Glaziers and Tin Plate Workers, 1532; Barkers and Tanners, 1547; Drapers and Tailors, 1549; Merchants or Mercers (incorporating Grocers 1345, Mercers 1393, Salters 1394, Ironmongers 1464 and Haberdashers 1467), 1561; Fullers and Feltmakers, 1565; Curriers and Tallow Chandlers, 1570; Free Masons, Rough Masons, Wallers, Slaters, Paviours, Plasterers and Bricklayers, 1594; Blacksmiths, Lorimers, Locksmiths, Cutlers, Bladesmiths and Girdlers, 1610; Saddlers and Upholsterers, 1659; Carpenters, Joiners, Wheelwrights, Sawyers and Coopers, 1661; Dyers and Listers, 1667.

All guild members had to take part in the annual celebration of the Feast of Corpus Christi, which took place on the Thursday after Trinity Sunday, one of Durham's great days when Town and Church came together. A record of one such procession was made in the late 16th century by a servant of the cathedral who remembered the days before the Dissolution in 1539. He records:

On that day the Town Bailiff would stand upon the Toll Booth in the Market Place and summon all the various guilds of trades and professions to get out their banners and torches and go to the north door of the Cathedral where they would form a line, banners to the west and torches on the east side of the path as far as Windy Gap. In the church of St Nicholas there was a fine shrine called the Corpus

61 *Kingsgate Bridge from the east.*

62 *Gateway into the College, looking out to the Baileys.*

Christi shrine which was carried in the procession. It was well gilded and had on its top a square container of Crystal in which the sacrament was kept. Four priests carried it up to Palace Green, preceded by a procession of people from all the churches in the town, until it came to rest at Windy Gap. Then St Cuthbert's Banner and two crosses led the procession of Prior and monks from the Cathedral to where it stood. Then the whole community, together with the choir knelt and prayed before the shrine. After the Prior had censed it, it was carried before the Prior, community and choir into the Cathedral where it was set up in the Choir. There followed a solemn service with the Te Deum sung, accompanied by the organ. All the guild banners followed the procession into the Cathedral where they processed round St Cuthbert's Feretory, their torches burning throughout the service. After the service the shrine was carried in procession back to St. Nicholas Church followed by all the banners. The shrine was then kept in the church vestry until the next year.

The shrine itself was destroyed by Dr Harvey, a commissioner during the Commonwealth, who was sent to the city for that specific purpose. He trod on it and it fell to pieces.

Also on Corpus Christi Day, members of the various guilds performed plays on Palace Green, dramas which were probably similar in style and content to the famous York Mystery Plays. Although the Corpus Christi Guild was eventually abolished by King Edward VI (1547-53), the ceremony itself lived on. After the Restoration of King Charles II in 1660, the Guild Procession took place annually on 29 May, known as Restoration or Oak Apple Day, and was continued until about 1770. The yearly blessing of the colliery banners in the cathedral on Durham Miners' Gala Day is

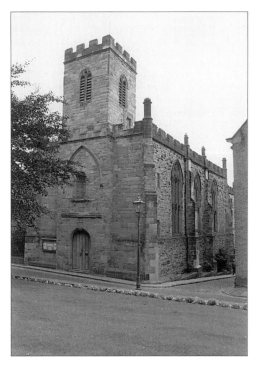

63 *St Mary-le-Bow, North Bailey, now a heritage centre.*

64 *Bow Lane from Kingsgate Bridge.*

perceived by some as a modern folk legacy of that great medieval guild procession.

Across Framwellgate Bridge from Silver Street, where South Street joins Crossgate, stands the church of St Margaret of Antioch, originally built in the 12th century as a chapel of ease to St Oswald's. In the shadow of the cathedral, the redundant church of St Mary-le-Bow, converted into a heritage centre in 1976, stands on the corner of the North Bailey's junction with Bow Lane. The original building is said to have been erected on the site of the shelter, the Tabernacle of Boughs, which housed St Cuthbert's body when it was first brought to Durham. Part of the medieval church and the old bailey gateway collapsed in 1637 but rebuilding, which did not even begin until about 1671, was completed in 1685. The west tower was erected in 1702.

The narrow, cobbled Bow Lane leads from the North Bailey through where the site of the old bailey gate stood to Kingsgate pedestrian bridge. During the 16th century, the river could be crossed here by Bow Bridge and, earlier, by a ford. It was down Bow Lane and across the ford that William the Conqueror is reputed to have fled, not stopping until he had crossed the Tees into North Yorkshire. Having insisted that Cuthbert's coffin should be opened so that he could see the body, he was suddenly seized by a strange illness and could not leave the area quickly enough.

65 *St Mary-the-Less, South Bailey.*

Across the street from the point where the North and South Bailey meet is the entrance to the College. The present gateway, built in about 1515 by Prior Castell, included St Helen's Chapel as its upper room and replaced a much earlier entrance to the monastery. Many of the buildings around the College green have medieval foundations and, before the Dissolution of the Monasteries, the Deanery used to be home to Durham's priors. The little church of St Mary-the-Less, tucked away opposite No. 4 South Bailey, has been the chapel of St John's College since 1919. The earlier church on this site dated from the 12th century when it was built by the Neville family. When rebuilding became necessary, in 1846, the architect used some of the stone from the previous church and probably followed its ground plan. Passage along Saddler Street was even more difficult before 1820 when a local landmark was demolished. The old North Gate which straddled Saddler Street and stood between nos. 49 and 50 was taken down. It had been the city gaol and was an extremely strong structure, its lower part having been defended by both a gate and a portcullis. It was the last of the medieval city gates to be removed. The gateway, rebuilt by Cardinal Langley, was often referred to as the gaol gate and was first used as a prison in 1424 on his instructions as he could no longer bear to see prisoners badly housed in a building on Palace Green. Records suggest that their lot was not greatly improved by the move and, certainly, their gaolers were an unsavoury crowd. A report on conditions in Durham Gaol in the 1770s includes observations that:

> The debtors have two damp, unhealthy rooms, 10 ft. 4 inches square. No sewers. At more than one of my visits I learned that the dirt, ashes etc. had lain there many months. The felons are put at night into dungeons, one 7 ft. square for three prisoners, another, the great hole, 16½ ft. by 12, has only a little window. In this I saw six prisoners chained to the floor. In that situation they had been for many weeks and were very sick. The straw on the floor was almost worn to dust. Commonside debtors in the low jail, whom I saw eating boiled bread and water, told me this was the only nourishment some had lived on for nearly twelve months. At several of my visits there were boys, thirteen and fifteen years of age, confined with the most profligate and abandoned.

The gate only allowed for the passage of traffic in one direction at a time and in 1773 all vehicles were stopped when the long-unused portcullis descended unexpectedly during repairs to the building. So heavily did it come down that it embedded itself deeply in the roadway and had to be cut to pieces to allow traffic to flow again.

Royal Mail coaches calling at Durham on their way from London to Edinburgh had to negotiate the narrow Saddler Street and the even more constricting North Gate as they made their way to the *Red Lion Inn* which stood in the North Bailey on the site now occupied by Hatfield College. The coach drivers must have been very relieved when the old prison was removed. It was last used as a prison in August 1819. By then the new gaol was ready in Old Elvet.

66 *The old Durham Gaol, Saddler Street.*

Another important feature of life in the Middle Ages was the mill where corn was ground. Durham has had eight such mills, two of them used for a time for the fulling (cleansing and thickening) of cloth. Two weirs on the river indicate where some of these mills stood. South Street Mill and the Old Fulling Mill (the latter originally two units, Jesus Mill and Lead Mill) are well known to today's visitor to Durham, although both are much changed from their original medieval appearance. Further downstream were the Bishop's Mill on the castle side of the river and the Clock Mill across from it. Of Kepier Mill no buildings now remain.

67   *Saddler Street, looking towards the cathedral.*

68   *The Old Fulling Mill.*

69   *South Street Mill, downstream from Prebends' Bridge.*

The monastery at Durham owned a great deal of property both within the city and further afield. One of its local holdings provided it with both food and income. Elvethall Manor, some of whose medieval buildings can still be seen behind Hallgarth Street, was farmed to provide crops of wheat, oats and barley. The diet of the monks at Durham seems to have been extremely good, and at the hospital established for 65 lepers at Sherburn provisions were also generous:

> Each leper was to have a loaf and a gallon of beer daily; three days in the week flesh meat, and four days fish; so that one dish of meat, fish, cheese, or butter, should serve two; but on great days, two dishes were to be provided, particularly on Quadragesima-day, when they were allowed fresh salmon, or other fish, if they could be had, for one dish; and on Michaelmas-day, they were to have geese, a goose to every four. They were allowed, yearly, three yards of woollen cloth, russet or white, six yards of linen, and six yards of canvas, with other necessaries, as trusses of straw and bundles of reeds.

On the banks of the River Wear, near to Frankland Prison, stand the quiet ruins of Finchale Priory. It was here in about 1110 that a hermit called Godric settled. Born in Walpole, Norfolk in 1065, he is said to have been a pedlar and a shipowner, travelling to such places as Spain, Rome and the Holy Land. Godric is also alleged to have engaged in piracy at some stage in his nautical career and to have had the blood of several men on his hands. It was supposedly on a journey to Lindisfarne that he heard about St Cuthbert and determined to follow in his footsteps, as far as that was possible. To start himself on this journey he travelled to Jerusalem. Forsaking the sea and back once more in England, he worked for some time in Norfolk before moving first to Carlisle and then to the small village of Wolsingham in Weardale, Co. Durham, where St Cuthbert told him in a vision that he was to go to Finchale although Godric did not know where that was. He spent some time at Whitby and then at the priory in Durham where, at last, he learned about Finchale, a bleak and deserted spot, infested with snakes it was said and often flooded. He lived at first about a mile up-river from the present ruins.

Godric's asceticism is well known. He is reputed to have habitually sat naked in the River Wear up to his neck all night long as a penance, to have worn nothing but sackcloth and to have eaten bread made of flour mixed with ashes and even then only when it was several months old. A little stone church was built during his lifetime to cater for the visitors who came to see him. Its foundations are within the chancel of the priory church and it was here that he was buried when he died in 1170, reputedly aged 105 years. It was Bishop Pudsey's son, Henry, who created a settlement here which in 1196 became a priory for eight monks. In the 14th century, Finchale really became a holiday home for the monks of Durham, four of them coming every three weeks to join the prior and his staff of four monks. Finchale Priory was one of the foundations hardest hit during Henry VIII's Dissolution of the Monasteries.

The ordinary citizens of medieval Durham would have risen with the sun and retired to bed with its setting; medieval artificial light was an expensive commodity. Their homes would have been cold and draughty in winter, hot and airless in summer. The streets they walked would have been smelly, muddy and unclean. They would have had to work long hours to make their livings and the threats of Scottish incursions, famine and disease were always present.

Crook Hall manor house seems to have started life in the 14th century, although some architectural historians believe it to have been begun in about 1286. The medieval hall is remarkable for its apparent originality. It is probable that the builder of the original property was Peter del Croke, hence Croke Hall. Joan del Croke married John de Copeland, the man who took prisoner the Scottish King David at the Battle of Neville's Cross. From the end of the 14th century until 1667 the property was owned by the Billingham family, one of whom was to have a serious argument with the citizens of Durham. In the 15th century the philanthropic Thomas Billingham allowed water from the Fram Well, which he owned, to be piped into Durham Market Place, and so it flowed for almost two centuries. In 1636 the supply suddenly dried up and on investigation it was found that Cuthbert Billingham, the owner of Crook Hall, had diverted the supply away from the city to power his mills. It transpired that an annual rent of some 13d. for the water had apparently not been paid and a lengthy legal battle ensued. A year later, however, the situation was resolved and the water supply resumed. Subsequent owners of Crook Hall were the Mickletons and the Hoppers, while a famous tenant was the 19th-century Durham historian, James Raine. A 17th-century extension links the old property to an 18th-century brick house of three storeys. The remaining part of the supposedly haunted staircase is believed to be the oldest set of wooden stairs in the county.

Eight

THE PILGRIMAGE OF GRACE
AND THE RISING OF THE NORTH

The time was rapidly approaching when the old order had to give way to the new and it was Cuthbert Tunstall who would both see out the old and ring in the new. Before he became Bishop of Durham, the see had been promised to Cardinal Campeggio to persuade him to hasten the divorce of Henry VIII from Queen Katharine. The cardinal was not, however, destined for Durham and, in the period before Tunstall was appointed, a yearly grant of £1,000 was made out of palatinate income to Anne Boleyn. Tunstall is thought by some to have been the illegitimate son of Sir Richard Tunstall of Thurland Castle in Lancashire but other historians argue that he was the son of Thomas, brother of Sir Richard. Tunstall became a priest in 1514 and rose to become Master of the Rolls and companion to Sir Thomas More on his ambassadorial duties. While still serving as a diplomat, often abroad, he was created, in 1522, Bishop of London and Keeper of the Great Seal.

He became Bishop of Durham in 1530, at a time when the consciences and beliefs of many were being tested to the full and a great change was about to take place in the religion of the country. In 1531 the clergy of England acknowledged that King Henry VIII was 'Supreme Head of the Church and Clergy' in place of the Pope, but the churchmen added the words 'so far as the law of Christ will allow'. Cuthbert Tunstall was one of those courageous enough to protest at what he regarded as the king's ill-advised move. In 1533 he was employed in attempting to persuade the queen to accept divorce from the king. In 1534, albeit reluctantly, he watched the passing of an Act of Parliament abolishing the Pope's spiritual authority in England and accepted the king's right to the title of 'Supreme Head on earth of the Church of England'. In 1535 the bishop was involved in an assessment of the value of Church livings and property in England. Between 1536 and 1539, Acts of Parliament were passed which, to all intents and purposes, abolished the monasteries of England. As a precursor to this, Henry VIII had sent out commissioners to enquire into the condition of the monasteries. These commissioners distorted the truth and, in some cases, simply told lies about what they found, but what they reported was precisely what the king wanted to hear. First to be closed down and their assets seized were more than three hundred religious houses with an annual value of less than £200.

The people of the north of England were fervent supporters of the 'old' religion and not at all happy about Henry's new order. They became even less happy when they saw the real results of what their king was doing. The poor and sick, who had for centuries received succour at the monasteries, were simply left to their own devices. Monks and nuns were left homeless and were themselves forced to beg for their food. The pill handed down by King Henry was just too big and too bitter for the people of the north to swallow. The result, in 1536, was the Pilgrimage of Grace. This was made, the northerners reasoned, 'for the love of God, for the restoring of faith, and for the restitution of the Church'. They made it clear that they were in no way threatening the king. The leader of the rebellion was a Yorkshire gentleman, Robert Aske, who was joined by the likes of Sir George Lumley, Sir John Bulmer, Sir Thomas Percy and the Archbishop of York. The large contingent initially reinstated the monks of Hexham to their abbey and then set off on a march southwards towards Doncaster. At the head of the procession were priests with crosses and men carrying banners depicting the crucified Christ. At Doncaster, the men of the north and the king's representatives who met them there came to an agreement that there would be an assembly in the north to consider grievances and that all who had taken part in the Pilgrimage of Grace would be pardoned for their actions. The people returned home but the king failed to keep his promises. The people rose again but this time the king's forces were ready for them, with the result that the rebels' attempts at taking Hull and Carlisle failed. Their leaders were captured. Robert Aske was executed at York, Sir John Bulmer, Sir Thomas Percy and Sir George Lumley suffered at Tyburn and Bulmer's wife was burned at Smithfield. Their followers were hanged in large numbers all over the northern counties.

An act was soon passed to remove all privileges from the palatinate. The bishop lost, at a stroke, the rights his predecessors had enjoyed for centuries. Cuthbert Tunstall had no choice but to submit in silence to the king's will. The 'Bishop's Peace', as it had been for centuries, became the 'King's Peace', which settled rather uneasily over Durham as the government of the great monastery was completely overhauled and passed over to a dean and prebendaries. In the process, the abbey at Durham, along with 13 others, became a collegiate body. Cuthbert Tunstall continued for the time being as Bishop of Durham but by the end of 1539 monastic life at Durham had come to an end. On 31 December that year:

> The prior, Hugh Whitehead, and convent, surrendered the monastery of Durham to the King. The whole of these institutions in Northumberland and Durham were suppressed, and their plate, revenues, and other property, taken possession of for the king. There were suppressed in England and Wales 643 monasteries, 90 colleges, 2,374 churches and free schools, and 110 hospitals.

On 1 May 1541 King Henry VIII granted a charter of foundation to the new cathedral, formerly the monastic church, at Durham to which he restored almost all the 'ancient possessions of the convent'.

In 1569 there was again religious unrest in the area, this time in a rebellion against Queen Elizabeth I. The 'Rising of the North', planned at the castles of Brancepeth and Raby, was an attempt to restore Roman Catholicism and to liberate Mary Queen of Scots:

> The rebels under the command of the earls of Westmorland and Northumberland entered Durham at the head of an armed force from Brancepeth, on the 14th of November, destroyed the books of common prayer and the bibles, and commanded mass to be sung in the cathedral. They immediately collected such forces as they could bring together, and marched by Darlington, Richmond, Northallerton, &c, to Wetherby, and mustered all their forces on Clifford Moor, amounting to three thousand eight hundred foot and about one thousand seven hundred horsemen. Whether from want of aid from other parts, want of money, or want of confidence in themselves, they suddenly retreated to the county of Durham, and besieged Barnard castle, which was held by Sir George Bowes for the queen. He sustained a siege for ten days; but from treachery within, and want of water, he was obliged to capitulate on honourable terms, and marched out with the garrison to join the Earl of Sussex who was advancing from York. They met at Sessay on the 12th December, and Sir George Bowes was appointed provost marshal of the army, which advanced to the county of Durham, backed by the army of the south, commanded by the Earl of Warwick and Lord Clinton. On their approach the earls disbanded their foot on the 16th December, and fled with their horse to Hexham and Naworth, where they were pursued, and they were obliged to take refuge in Scotland. The estates of the principal rebels were confiscated. Forty constables, with alderman Struther, parson Plumtree, and several citizens, were executed in the market place at Durham, on the 6th January. The Earl of Westmorland escaped to Flanders, and died in poverty at Newport in 1601. The Earl of Northumberland was imprisoned at Loughleven and sold for £2000 ... to Queen Elizabeth, and he was brought to York, where he was executed on the 22nd August, 1572.
> (M.A. Richardson, *Local Historian's Table Book*, 1846)

In 1589, twenty years after this disastrous attempt at a coup, while Roman Catholic priests and their supporters were still illegally active in the area, the plague began to wreak havoc in the North East. By July 1597 the disease was claiming lives:

> At Newcastle, and the following places in the county of Durham: Durham, Darlington, Gateshead, Whickham, Stainton, Burdon, Boldon, Houghton, Chester, Billingham, St. Helen Auckland, Wolsingham, Aycliffe, and in several other places. The poor inhabitants of the city of Durham, were lodged in huts erected upon the moors near that place. Bishop Mathew [Matthew] retired to his castle at Stockton to avoid the infection. October 17, there were dead of the plague at Darlington, three hundred and forty

70 *J.M.W. Turner's view of Durham Cathedral and Castle from Prebends' Bridge.*

persons. October 27, there was dead in Elvet, in the city of Durham, more than four hundred; in St. Nicholas' parish one hundred; in St. Margaret's two hundred; in St. Giles' sixty; in St. Mary's in the North Bailey, sixty. Twenty-four prisoners died in gaol. Two hundred and fifteen deaths are recorded in the parish of St. Nicholas, Durham, between the 11th of July and the 27th of November. Many of these persons were buried on the moor, or in St. Thomas's chapel, beyond Claypath. (M.A. Richardson, *Local Historian's Table Book*, 1846)

In January and February 1598 the plague 'ceased' but broke out again on 15 September. In 1604, it came once more to the parish of St Giles in Durham City, its last recorded appearance in the city.

Nine

CIVIL WAR AND COMMONWEALTH

The City of Durham had been successful in obtaining a charter from the Crown but Bishop Matthew went to a great deal of expense to have it quashed on the grounds that it was an infringement of his franchise. Put more simply, he did not want the Crown interfering in the affairs of the bishopric. Then, on 21 September 1602, the bishop himself granted a charter to the city. In future, Durham's affairs would be supervised by a mayor and aldermen instead of by a bailiff as had previously been the case. The first elected Mayor of Durham, James Farrales, was in place by 4 October 1602 and it was not long before the city welcomed England's new monarch, King James I, who was making his way from Scotland to London:

> 1603 April the 13th, his majesty arrived at the city of Durham, where he was received by the magistrates, and afterwards entertained in the castle by the bishop, who attended him with a hundred gentlemen in tawny livery coats. Next day his majesty left the castle, and slept that night at Walworth house [Walworth Castle, to the west of Darlington], at that time the residence of Mrs. Jennison, widow of Thomas Jennison, Esq.

In 1617 James returned to Durham, this time on his long journey to Scotland:

> April 17. King James I on his progress into Scotland, arrived at Auckland palace and remained there till the 19th. On the 18th [Good Friday], one of his majesty's footmen named Master Heaburne, arrived in the city of Durham, and signified to George Walton, esq., mayor, that it was his majesty's pleasure to enter that place in state on the 19th, Easter eve. The king came in by Elvet, and the mayor, mounted on horseback, received him on Elvet bridge. Master Heaburne took his station near the mayor and aldermen, until the king's arrival, when a loyal speech was delivered by the mayor, who surrendered to his majesty the staff and mace, and also presented in the name of the city, a silver bowl, gilt with a cover. After having delivered his speech, the mayor was directed by Master Heaburne to remount his horse and ride before his majesty, when having proceeded a few yards, a stop was made, whilst an apprentice recited some verses to his majesty. The mayor was then placed next the sword, and so bearing the city mace, rode before the king to the cathedral. On Easter Monday the king rode to see a horse-race on Woodham moor [near the modern Newton Aycliffe], and returned to Durham, and on the Tuesday, the 22d, being St. George's day he continued his progress to Newcastle … (M.A. Richardson, *Local Historian's Table Book*, 1846)

It was James I who, in 1624, finally abolished the right of sanctuary in England.

His son, King Charles I, had first passed through County Durham as a child, following his father to London and staying as a guest of the Bishop of Durham at Auckland Castle. Thirty years later he stayed there again, this time as King of England:

71 *Almsdish, part of the Auckland Castle plate, by Wolfgang Howzer, 17th-century.*

72 *A standing paten, part of the cathedral plate, 17th-century.*

1633 (May) King Charles I, on his progress to Scotland, was entertained at Raby castle, by sir Henry Vane; and from thence came, on Friday the last of May, to Auckland castle, where he was entertained by bishop Morton. The next day Saturday, 1st of June he came to Durham, where a way was made thro' at Elvet head, that he might ride thro' into the city; and there he mounted his horse and was mett by sir William Belasyse, high sheriff, and the gentlemen of the county, who gave all the sheriff's livery, two hundred men; viz. ash-coloured cloth lined with red bays and plush capes, four fingers broad, and two broad silver laces. As soon as his majesty lighted, he went first to the Abbey church, before he went to the castle; a canopy of state was borne over him by eight prebendarys into the church, where he staid [for the] service; and a speech was made to him by Dean Hunt. Then his majesty went to the castle; and on Sunday morning heard a sermon at the Abbey from the bishop, where none were admitted but his nobles, the clergy, and choir. After service he dined at the Deanery at the bishop's charge, where his majesty had a cope that cost £140, belonging to the church, presented to him. Then he attended evening prayer; and after went to the castle, where he kept his court during all the time he was at Durham, and did touch divers for the king's evil. Dr. Cosins, one of the prebendaries, was sworn one of the king's chaplains. And on Monday morning his majesty went to Newcastle. (M.A. Richardson, *Local Historian's Table Book*, 1846)

While the king and his retinue were at Durham, they were entertained by the bishop at a cost of £1,500 a day. It was during Charles I's stay at the castle that Dicky Pearson, the bishop's jester or fool, on seeing the Earl of Pembroke 'richly and fantastically dressed', went up to him and said, 'I am the Bishop of Durham's fool; whose fool are you?' The earl's reply is not recorded.

In 1639 the king again passed through Durham:

April 29. King Charles I on his march against the Scots covenanters, left York, and arrived the same night at Raby castle, in the county of Durham, the seat of sir Henry Vane, treasurer of his majesty's household, where he was nobly entertained. From thence he went to Durham, where bishop Morton, with great expressions of joy and welcome, entertained his majesty during his stay there. The king remained at Durham, while the horse and foot intended to be levied there, were raised and upon their march. (M.A. Richardson, *Local Historian's Table Book*, 1846)

On 30 August 1640 the Scottish covenanters defeated the English army at the Battle of Newburn and soon occupied both Newcastle and Durham. Even before they arrived, Durham had suffered at the hands of the English soldiers as they retreated into Yorkshire:

As for the city of Durham it became a most depopulated place; not one shop for four days after the fight open; not one house in ten that had either man, woman, or child, in it; not one bit of bread to be got for money, for the king's army had eat and drank all in their march into Yorkshire; the country people durst not come to market, which made that city in a sad condition for want of food. After the defeat of the royal troops at Newburn, the bishop of Durham fled to his castle at Stockton, and from thence retired to York and London. The castle remained for some time in the possession of the royalists.

August 30, the Scots entered Durham. The earl of Strafford issued an order from Darlington to cause all such quantities of butter, bread, cheese, and milk, as could be possibly furnished, to be brought into Darlington by four o'clock the next day for victualling his majesty's army; to break or bury all the upper mill-stones, and to remove the goods, and drive the cattle before the approach of the Scots. (M.A. Richardson, *Local Historian's Table Book*, 1846)

The Scots left the area in 1641 but only when they had been paid £60,000 by King Charles to do so and after having used Durham Cathedral as a barracks.

At the end of the Civil War between King and Parliament, Durham and the other bishoprics in the country were at the mercy of the new Puritan regime:

1646 October 9. An ordinance for the total abolition of episcopacy passed both houses of parliament, and was followed, on the 16th of November, by an order for the sale of bishops' lands. The total amount of lands, belonging to the see of Durham, sold by virtue of this ordinance was £68,121-15s-9d. (M.A. Richardson, *Local Historian's Table Book*, 1846)

In February 1647 King Charles arrived in Durham as the prisoner of the English Parliament, having been bought from the Scots for the sum of £20,000, a fee which also guaranteed the withdrawal of the Scottish army from England. On his way from Newcastle-upon-Tyne to London, he was closely guarded by Parliamentary commissioners.

In 1649 the bishopric was deprived of one of its most ancient assets:

May 2. Durham castle was sold to Thomas Andrews, lord mayor of London, for £1267-0s-10d, who so miserably defaced a great part of it, that it was some time before it could be made habitable for bishop Cosin, who almost renovated it by making considerable alterations and additions. (M.A. Richardson, *Local Historian's Table Book*, 1846)

On 14 July 1650, Oliver Cromwell was in Durham on his way to the Battle of Dunbar:

Oliver Cromwell, general of the parliament army, arrived at Durham, where he was met by sir Arthur Haslerigg, governor of Newcastle, with colonel Pride and other officers, who attended him to that town [Newcastle] on the day following. (M.A. Richardson, *Local Historian's Table Book*, 1846)

After the battle, Durham Cathedral was the unlikely prison to which thousands of Scots were taken:

> After the fight at Dunbar, General Cromwell sent a great number of the prisoners taken on that occasion to Newcastle, recommending them to be treated with humanity. The following passages occur concerning these prisoners, in a letter from sir Arthur Haslerigg, to the council of state, dated at Newcastle, October 31, 1650. 'When they came to Morpeth, the prisoners being put into a large walled garden, they eat up raw cabbages, leaves and roots … which cabbage (they having fasted, as they themselves said, near eight days) poisoned their bodies; for, as they were coming from thence to Newcastle, some died by the way-side. When they came to Newcastle, I put them into the greatest church in the town; and the next morning, when I sent them to Durham, about one hundred and forty were sick, and not able to march. Three died that night, and some fell down on their march from Newcastle to Durham, and died. On being told into the great cathedral church, they were counted to be no more than three thousand, although colonel Fenwick, wrote me that there were three thousand, five hundred. While lodged in the cathedral the Scotch prisoners sadly mutilated the Neville and other monuments; and are said to have warmed themselves at a huge fire made of the wooden stall work of the choir. It is further said that most of them perished and dyed there in a very short space, and were thrown into holes by great numbers together in a most lamentable manner. (M.A. Richardson, *Local Historian's Table Book*, 1846)

In 1651 still more of the bishopric's land was sold off, this time Framwellgate and the Old Borough, bought by the Corporation of Durham for £200. In 1652 Durham saw yet another innovation:

> July 5. The county of Durham, which in consequence of its palatinate privileges, had hitherto never sent knights or burgesses to parliament, found representatives in Cromwell's three parliaments, viz. at the above period, Henry Davison for the county. In 1654, September 3, Robert Lilburne, of Thickley, esq., and George Lilburne, of Sunderland, esq. In 1656, September 17, Thomas Lilburne, of Offerton, esq., and James Clavering, of Axwell, esq., Anthony Smith, alderman, represented the city of Durham in both of the latter parliaments. (M.A. Richardson, *Local Historian's Table Book*, 1846)

In 1657, Parliament having been petitioned on the matter three times by people in Durham County, Oliver Cromwell approached the Speaker of the House of Commons advocating the conversion of several old chapter houses at Durham Cathedral into a college. He argued for the scheme on the grounds that it would do much to promote 'learning and piety in these poore, rude and ignorant parts'. It called for an establishment comprising a provost, two senior fellows, four professors, four tutors and four schoolmasters for 24 scholars and 12 exhibitioners. Perceiving the potential threat, the vice-chancellor of Oxford University sent embassies to London to object most strongly, but he need not have worried because the death of Oliver Cromwell in 1658, the end of the Commonwealth and the return of the monarchy ended the venture.

In November 1660 King Charles II was restored to the throne, an event celebrated in Durham City as elsewhere. The bishopric of Durham was handed to John Cosin who began to restore Durham Castle, so severely damaged during the time it was owned by the Lord Mayor of London. Cosin is the bishop remembered for his love of anything which could be created in wood, as many churches in the diocese bear witness, with fine examples of carving ordered by him. When he became bishop he was already 66 and had spent many years in exile but, despite having to oversee the restoration of everyday Church of England life in the cathedral and the diocese, he

73 *Seventeenth-century Italian altar frontal, part of the 'Treasures of St Cuthbert' exhibition.*

made it his business to restore the fabric of the churches in his care. At Bishop Auckland, from Hugh Pudsey's old banqueting hall, he created the graceful building which Sir Timothy Eden called the most beautiful private chapel in England. In his repairs to Durham Castle he built the famous black staircase. He saw to the chancel. On Palace Green, he erected a new library and placed in it a wonderful collection of books. He restored the schools built by Bishop Langley and established, also beside the Green, a hospital for eight poor people. In Durham City's market place he was heavily involved in the rebuilding of the Guildhall.

Durham City sent its first members of Parliament to London in 1678. They were Sir Ralph Cole of Brancepeth Castle, who polled 408 votes, and John Parkhurst from Northamptonshire with 379.

Approximately where 39 Silver Street now stands, there was, until 1964, a house which was once home to one of Durham's most famous residents, Sir John Duck. He was a man who reputedly owed his good luck to a raven. Not himself a native of Durham, he came to the city as a young man. He was born in 1634, probably at Kilton in North Yorkshire since in his will he specifically mentions the poor of that village. The young Duck appears to have arrived in Durham without a penny to his name, looking for employment as a butcher's apprentice. Since he was not a member of the Butchers' Guild, however, he found that was no easy matter. After several fruitless attempts to contact someone who would give him the opportunity to demonstrate his worth, he met a butcher called John Heslop who, contrary to guild practice, accepted him as his apprentice. The wedding of Ann Heslop, his employer's daughter or sister, and John Duck was performed in the presence of the Mayor of Durham, John Airson, at St Nicholas' church in the market place on 30 July 1655.

While all seemed initially to be going well, the future for the couple was not straightforward. John Heslop had obviously offended other guild members by employing Duck, as demonstrated by a record in the books of the Incorporated Company of Butchers of the City of Durham:

> Memorandum. That on Tuesday, 12th January, 1656, being one of the quarter meetinge dayes, Robert Blunt and Clement Ladler, Wardens of this Company of Butchers gave John Heslopp warning that from henceforth hee forebeare to sett John Duck on work in the trade of a butcher upon payne for every default 39s. 11d. (M.A. Richardson, *Local Historian's Table Book*, 1846)

Heslop was going to have to dismiss his apprentice but, rather than involve his father-in-law in further argument with the guild, John Duck decided himself that his future lay elsewhere and made plans to leave Durham. Fate then intervened in a most remarkable way. The story is told that Duck was on the banks of the River Wear, walking towards Framwellgate Bridge to make his way out of the city, when he observed a raven flying above him with something shiny in its beak. As he walked the bird followed him, and when he was crossing the bridge it swooped low and released the gold coin it had been carrying. He watched the bird fly away and then bent down to retrieve the money. As he was examining it, a farmer berating the two cows he was attempting to drive approached him across the bridge. Asking what the problem was, Duck learned that the man had been having trouble

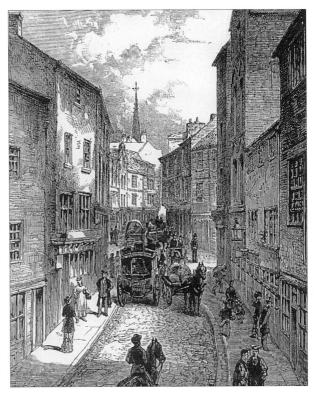

74   *Silver Street in the 1880s.*

with the animals all day. They struck a bargain, and he exchanged his coin for the two troublesome creatures which he soon sold, at a profit, in the market place. Giving up all thought of starting life anew elsewhere, John Duck used the profit to continue dealing in cattle. Despite not having completed his apprenticeship and facing possible opposition from the guild, he also began to trade as a butcher.

He gradually made a great deal of money and, as is often the way, became a highly respected citizen. In 1680 John Duck was not only installed as Mayor of the City of Durham but was given the freedom of the Butchers Company:

> John Duck Esq. Maior of the Cittie of Durham is admitted with the consent of the Company a freeman of the Fraternity of Butchers, and have paid for such his said admission 13s 4d.
> (M.A. Richardson, *Local Historian's Table Book*, 1846)

He used some of his wealth to buy an estate at Haswell. He also became the owner of several coal mines and leased others from the Church at Durham. He made money in this new venture and in 1686 was created a baronet by King James II. He founded a hospital at Great Lumley and it was at this time that he and his wife moved into the Silver Street house. Both Sir John Duck and his wife were buried in Durham's St Margaret's church. He died in 1691 at the age of 59 while Ann died in 1695.

Ten

THE EIGHTEENTH-CENTURY CITY

The principal aim of the first Jacobite Rebellion in 1715 was to replace the new Hanoverian King of England, George I, with James Edward Stuart, son of the former King James II. There were risings in support of James Edward, the 'Old Pretender', in Scotland and the north of England. One of the leaders of the English revolt was James Radcliffe, 3rd Earl of Derwentwater, whose home was Dilston Hall near Corbridge in Northumberland. The rebellion failed and, for his involvement, Derwentwater paid with his life:

> James, earl of Derwentwater, was beheaded on Tower-hill, Feb. 24, 1716. Of all the victims who perished in this rash enterprise, none fell more lamented than the young and generous earl of Derwentwater. It is generally supposed that the unfortunate earl's last request, that of burial with his ancestors was refused, and that the body was interred in the church yard of St. Giles', Holborn. However, either a sham burial took place, or the corpse was afterwards removed, for it was certainly carried secretly by his friends, resting by day and travelling only by night, into Northumberland, and deposited with the remains of his father in the chapel at Dilston. Tradition still points out Whitesmocks, near the city of Durham, as one of the places where the corpse rested, thus avoiding that city. (M.A. Richardson, *Local Historian's Table Book*, 1846)

In 1745, when the Jacobites embarked on a second rebellion, this time with the 'Young Pretender', Bonnie Prince Charlie, as their figurehead, Durham, both city and county, demonstrated their support for the Hanoverians. Troops were mustered on the surrounding moors and cavalrymen were lodged in the city itself. In January 1746 the Duke of Cumberland arrived in Durham to be greeted at Elvet by the mayor, aldermen, banners and bands. Cumberland was subsequently instrumental in defeating the rebels at the Battle of Culloden. People who live in the North East are frequently referred to as 'Geordies', probably because during the rebellions of 1715 and 1745 they were, essentially, supporters of George I and then George II. In this part of the country anyone called George is usually nicknamed Geordie, and even kings were treated no differently.

Proposals to enhance transport and commerce in the city were being put forward at this time. The statue of Neptune, restored to its market place site in 1991, had originally been given to the city in 1729 by George Bowes, M.P. of Gibside and Streatlam, as a symbol of the scheme to link Durham City to the sea by improved navigation of the River Wear. Over time, four such schemes were proposed, none

75 *King George I, after the portrait by Sir Godfrey Kneller.*

76 *Early photograph of statue of Neptune on the market place pant, or fountain.*

of which came to fruition. At first the statue stood on top of the market place well-heads, very close to its present site, but found a new home in 1863 on top of E.R. Robson's replacement well-head fountain. The old man of the sea also topped the new pant, or fountain, of 1902. In 1923 the statue was moved to Durham's Wharton Park from where it was removed, having been struck by lightning, for restoration in 1986 by Andrew Naylor of Telford.

Beyond the market place, just across the road from *The Shakespeare Inn* in Durham's steep and narrow Saddler Street, is a vennel, or alley, called Drury Lane. As might be supposed, it has theatrical connections because behind 43 and 44 Saddler Street from 1722 until at least the end of the 18th century there was a theatre. Diagonally opposite, behind no. 61, another theatre existed from 1792. This one survived, although much changed and used latterly as a warehouse, into the middle of the 20th century. There was another theatre in Hallgarth Street in 1760.

The first of the two Saddler Street theatres was described in 1722 as 'a very handsome Play-house built fit for the Reception of Quality and Gentry'. In 1746 the

77 *The restored statue of Neptune in the market place.*

property was listed as having 'a Cock-Pit and Playhouse'. In 1754, John Richardson leased the site and eventually built a new theatre there which opened on 10 July 1771:

> The new theatre in the city of Durham was opened with *The West Indian*, and other entertainments, to a very genteel audience, who expressed the greatest satisfaction at the elegance of the house, and of the performance in general. (M.A. Richardson, *Local Historian's Table Book*, 1846)

One of the players at this theatre was James Cawdell who, in 1782, became manager of the company which acted there. When he was refused permission to continue to lease the property, he decided to build a new and larger theatre just across Saddler Street. It was begun in grand style:

> 6th July, 1791 – The foundation stone of a new theatre was laid in the city of Durham with great masonic eclat by George Finch, esq., deputy grand master for the county, in the presence of Thomas Chipchase, esq., mayor, and William Ambler, esq., recorder of the city. A plate, with a suitable inscription, was deposited within the stone. (M.A. Richardson, *Local Historian's Table Book*, 1846)

The building was obviously erected fairly quickly because the next entry about the new theatre records that on:

> March 12th, 1792, this theatre was opened with an occasional prelude, called *Apollo's Holiday*, written by Mr. Cawdell, the new comedy of *Wild Oats*, and the farce of *The Spoiled Child*. (M.A. Richardson, *Local Historian's Table Book*, 1846)

Mr Cawdell used his talents as a writer for the public good. On 22 March 1793, in order to help to raise funds for the new Durham Infirmary;

78   *Entrance to Drury Lane in Saddler Street.*

The tragedy of *Cato* was represented at the theatre, Durham, to assist the funds of this institution; the parts of Cato and Juba being performed by W. Eddis and W. Smith esqrs., of that city, which characters they supported throughout with great success. An excellent prologue was written for the occasion by Mr. Cawdell, the manager, and admirably delivered by him. The house was full in every part, and the sum of fifty guineas was paid into the hands of the treasurer of the Infirmary.

Cawdell died at his house in the South Bailey in 1800, and the theatre he had built was leased from then until 1806 to Stephen Kemble, undoubtedly the most illustrious name associated with the Durham theatre. He was a member of the great 18th-century acting family, brother to Charles and John Philip Kemble. Their sister was Mrs Sarah Siddons, Britain's leading actress of the time, who occasionally appeared in the Durham theatre while Stephen was managing it. His wife, Elizabeth Satchell Kemble, was also an actress. Stephen Kemble, known for being able to play the part of *Falstaff* without needing to wear padding, died on 6 June 1822:

Died, at the Grove, near Durham, in his 64th year, Stephen George Kemble, esq., the celebrated comedian, and formerly manager of the theatres-royal of Newcastle, Glasgow, and Edinburgh. Mr. Kemble, who was a very corpulent man, had retired for some years from the exercise of the laborious profession of an actor. In many characters he was confessedly unrivalled; and it is no small commendation that he was considered by the late Mr. Sheridan to be the best declaimer he had ever heard on or off the stage. He was also possessed of considerable literary talents.

ESTABLISHED 1692.

AINSLEY'S CELEBRATED DURHAM MUSTARD,

MANUFACTURED SOLELY AT THE ORIGINAL ESTABLISHMENT,

22, FOOT OF SILVER-STREET, DURHAM,

BY

JOHN BALMBROUGH,

Sole Proprietor and only Successor to the late Joseph William Ainsley (and to the Business for so many years carried on by his present wife, then Eleanor Ainsley, and who is the last and only survivor of the Family of Joseph Wm. Ainsley, who first manufactured the Article.

79   *Early advertisement for Durham mustard.*

Near the entrance to Saddlers Yard, off Saddler Street, was a property where, in 1720, a Mrs Clements, or Clemens, reputedly first developed a revolutionary new method of grinding the heart of mustard seeds to produce an extremely fine powder which could be kept, dry, for a comparatively long period of time. Before her discovery, mustard was kept by being rolled up into little balls with cinammon and honey. When needed for use, these were mixed with vinegar. In its day this 'Durham mustard' was famed throughout the land and King George I is said to have been one of its keenest users. So popular was the product that many local farmers took to growing mustard as a main crop. One such farm was at Houghall, between Durham and Shincliffe. The product is commemorated in an old Durham saying: 'The City of Durham is famous for seven things – Wood, Water and Pleasant Walks, Law and Gospel, Old Maids and Mustard.'

There is a suggestion that Durham mustard was first manufactured in 1692. There were eventually three mustard factories in Durham: William Ainsley's was in Saddler Street and then Waddington Street; John Balmbrough's occupied a site at the foot of Silver Street, while Simpson and Willan operated in Gilesgate. Colman's bought the last of these factories in 1897.

Granville Sharp, born in the city in 1735, was an indefatigable fighter against slavery. It was largely due to his constant campaigning that slavery was made illegal in Britain in 1772. Co-founder and first chairman of the British and Foreign Bible Society, he died in London in 1813.

On the corner of Bow Lane, a site now occupied by part of St Chad's College, there used to stand a cottage which was the home until 1780 of the Porter family, including the children William Ogilvie, Jane, Robert and Anna Maria. Although all were born in Durham they left as very young children following the death in 1779 of their father, William, an army surgeon. They moved to Edinburgh where they formed an association with Flora Macdonald, by then a celebrity, who had aided the escape from Scotland of Bonnie Prince Charlie after the failed Jacobite Rebellion of 1745, and died in 1790. This link is supposed to have fostered the children's love of romance.

Jane was given to rising very early every morning and, as a child, read Spenser's *Faerie Queene*. She loved to write and always seemed to be deep in thought. Her first novel, written when she was 27, was *Thaddeus of Warsaw*, an historical novel published in 1803 and translated into several languages. In 1810 she chronicled, rather romantically, the life of William Wallace in *The Scottish Chiefs*. She also found success with her stories *The Pastor's Fireside* and *The Field of Forty Footsteps*, as well as collaborating with her sister Anna Maria in 1826 to produce *Tales Round a Winter's Hearth*. Anna Maria, like Jane, was educated in Edinburgh, where a frequent visitor to the Porter home was the young Walter Scott. Nicknamed L'Allegra because of her cheerful disposition, Anna Maria was just 13 when she started to write *Artless Tales*, published two years later, but she is best remembered for her novel of the French Revolutionary war, *The Hungarian Brothers*.

80   *Victorian Durham from the north-west, by R.W. Billings.*

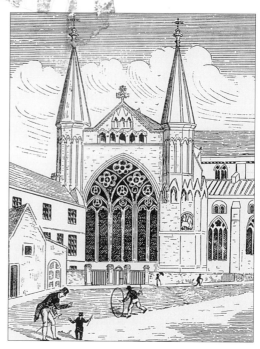

81   *Count Boruwlaski, the Polish dwarf.*

82   *Count Boruwlaski in conversation in the cathedral yard.*

One of Anna Maria and Jane's brothers would become Sir Robert Ker Porter, who is buried in St Petersburg and to whom there is a monument in Bristol Cathedral. Born in 1777, he was an artist, a writer and a diplomat as well as a *bon viveur*, a generally dashing character and friend of both Scott and Turner. He studied for two years at the Royal Academy in London and found fame as a painter of battle scenes, often on huge canvases. One of his enormous circular 'panoramas', *The Conquest of Mysore*, exhibited in 1800, was seven metres high and 40 metres long and was described as one of the wonders of the world. At the age of 25 he was commissioned a captain in the Westminster Militia but was persuaded against pursuing a military career and a year later was appointed Historical Painter to the Czar of Russia. While in Russia, he fell in love with Princess Mary von Scherbatoff whom he married in 1812. In 1806 he was knighted by King Gustavus IV of Sweden and three years later published his *Travelling Sketches in Russia and Sweden*. He had been present at the Battle of Coruña with Sir John Moore and, in 1813, was knighted by the Prince Regent. He also received honours from the ruler of Persia and, in 1826, the year during which his wife died of typhus, was appointed British Consul in Venezuela. While in South America, he painted a fine portrait of Simon Bolivar, after whom Bolivia, formerly Upper Peru, was named. Sir Robert Ker Porter died in Russia in 1842.

The least well known of the Porter children was the eldest, William Ogilvie. He was a naval surgeon and novelist, and a good number of his letters are held among the Archives and Special Collections of Durham University Library. They were bought from Sotheby's in 1967.

Joseph Boruwlaski, referred to even today as 'the Polish dwarf', was buried in the cathedral, but his memorial was erected in the church of St Mary-the-Less because the style and wording of it were felt to be inappropriate to the great church. Boruwlaski was famous primarily for his size. He was just 39 inches tall when fully grown and, although always something of a curiosity, established himself as a respected member of Durham society. Born near Chaliez in Poland in 1739, he was one of six children of perfectly normally proportioned parents. Three of the offspring grew to a normal size while the others remained unusually small. Although Joseph was so small, his body was perfectly proportioned. The Boruwlaski family had once been quite wealthy but Joseph's father died when the boy was only nine years old. A friend of the family, Countess Humieski [sometimes Humiecka or Humieska], 'adopted' him and, when he was 15 and not yet three feet tall, took him on a tour of the courts of Europe. He was regarded as something of a sensation and was fêted everywhere he went. He became used to mingling with monarchs and courtiers and was renowned for his tact and courtesy.

On one occasion, as he notes in his memoirs, he was presented to the Empress Maria Theresa, who sat him on her knee. Noticing that Joseph was gazing at her hand, the empress thought that he was looking at the fine ring she was wearing. She offered it to him but he explained that it was not the ring but her hand at which he had been staring and asked leave to kiss it. The empress was so charmed that she removed her ring and tried to fit it onto the little man's finger but it just slipped off. She then called over a six-year-old girl who was herself wearing a very attractive ring. Having asked the child for it, she slipped it onto Boruwlaski's finger. He treasured the gift all his life for the child who had owned the ring was Marie Antoinette, who became the ill-fated wife of Louis XVI of France and was to lose her head before the century was out.

When Boruwlaski was 25, he fell in love with a French actress. His love was unrequited, however, and he returned to Poland and the countess who sheltered him. For almost 15 years he remained with her but then fell in love with a woman called Isalina Barboutan, companion to the countess. When she discovered the romance, she sent Isalina back home and locked Boruwlaski in his room for two weeks. On his release he was informed in no uncertain terms that he had two choices, either to remain with the countess or to leave her house forever. He chose the latter course but was deeply upset at having to leave the person who had shown him so much kindness. Not having enough money to support his Isalina, Boruwlaski approached the ruler of Poland, who awarded him a pension, but despite such generosity Boruwlaski was still short of money. He decided that, for the first time

83 *Prebends' Bridge.*

84 *The Watergate looking back into South Bailey.*

85 *Prebends' Bridge, looking downstream.*

86   *Sir Walter Scott's famous words on Prebends' Bridge.*

in his life, he would have to earn a living. His only obvious skill was as a violinist and so he embarked on yet another tour of the European courts looking for a new patron. In 1782 he was presented at the English court and met the Duke of Gloucester who befriended him. Sadly, both the duke and another new friend died, leaving the Pole again to fend for himself.

He determined to make a new start in America but, before he could sail, two women gave him enough money to remain in England. Boruwlaski left London and settled, eventually, in Durham, where he shared the home of his great friend Mr Ebdon and his family in The Grove. He was very popular with cathedral society, several of whose members had special cutlery made for him to use when he dined with them. Boruwlaski once wrote:

> Poland was my cradle,
> England is my nest.
> Durham is my quiet place,
> Where my bones shall rest.

87   *Some of the cathedral plate, mainly 18th-century.*

When he died in September 1837 he was 97 years old and was buried in the cathedral to the west of the north door. His grave is simply marked with the initials J B.

In 1771 Durham City suffered what was probably the worst of the many floods it has experienced:

> The water at Durham was eight feet ten inches higher than ever known before; two houses at the end of Framwellgate bridge were entirely swept away; one of the abbey mills, and the bridge belonging to the dean and chapter were demolished, as were four arches of Elvet bridge, and all the lower buildings of the city, garden walls, &c., were either destroyed or left in a ruinous condition. Mrs. Morgan's house, and Mr. Wilkinson's coachhouse, both in Elvet, were driven down by the water, but the houses behind prevented them being carried off. Many other houses were greatly damaged; several horses, cows, &c., were drowned in the stables, byers, &c. Happily no lives were lost there, though a young woman fell into the water, by the bank giving way, and was carried 700 yards down the river, yet was saved by the assistance of her fellow servant. The whole of the low grounds near Finchale abbey were wholly under water. (M.A. Richardson, *Local Historian's Table Book*, 1846)

One of the results of the flood was that Durham City gained one of its most famous landmarks, Prebends Bridge, which offers probably the best-known view of Durham Cathedral. From the South Bailey, access can be gained to it through the Water Gate, an arch built by the Rev. Henry Egerton in 1778 to replace a medieval gateway. The three-arched Prebends Bridge of 1777 was designed by George Nicholson to replace that of 1696 destroyed by the deluge. An earlier footbridge had facilitated the crossing of the Wear from 1574. At the south end of Prebends Bridge is an inscription bearing Sir Walter Scott's immortal lines:

> Grey towers of Durham
> Yet well I love thy mixed and massive piles
> Half church of God half castle' gainst the Scot
> And long to roam these venerable aisles
> With records stored of deeds long since forgot.

The cathedral was seriously threatened and much damaged in the late 18th century by men who felt that they were doing the right thing. In the 1770s a local architect, John Wooler, informed the Dean and Chapter that the cathedral was in an alarmingly dangerous condition. Virtually every part of the building, he suggested, was in need of urgent repair. His assistant, George Nicholson, having just finished his work on Prebends Bridge, began to 'restore' the fabric, chiselling deep into the exterior walls and removing windows, this work subsequently being continued by James Wyatt. Wyatt demolished practically all of the beautiful Norman chapter house and planned to pull down the Galilee Chapel to make way for a carriage drive up to the great west door, which he proposed to reopen. Before this project was actually terminated, he had already removed the lead from the roof. He had also wanted to erect a spire on the central tower and to raise the floor level of the Chapel of the Nine Altars to that of the rest of the cathedral. Neither proposal was allowed to proceed.

Eleven

Nineteenth-Century People

In the late 18th and early 19th centuries, many of the Durham clergy were wealthy in comparison with their counterparts elsewhere. This was largely because of the revenue derived from the coal deposits beneath the Church's land. Some Durham clergymen held other livings as well as those in the county, a system known as 'plurality', thus achieving even greater incomes. Along with the outcry for parliamentary reform came a call for the overhaul of what was perceived to be this iniquitous system. Also to come under close scrutiny was the income, or reported income, of the Bishop of Durham. Some of the Durham clergy were aware of the storm about to break over them and decided they were best advised to do nothing and await the thunder, while others felt that action needed to be taken immediately to retain at least some of the Church funds within the county and to appropriate them for good purpose.

One of those who shared this latter vision was Bishop William van Mildert, an opponent of parliamentary reform, who had ascended the episcopal throne in 1826 as successor to Shute Barrington. It was in July 1831 that van Mildert and others conceived the idea of diverting Church funds into the creation of a University of Durham. It was later claimed there were few Church supporters of the new scheme but at the time it received enthusiastic support from a lot of people. The bishop was asked by some to lower his academic sights but argued that nothing less than 'a university with the power of granting degrees' would answer the expectations of the public. On 4 July 1832 the Royal Assent was given to the bill for the establishment of a university at Durham, 'An act to enable the dean and chapter of Durham to appropriate part of the property of their church to the establishment of a university in connexion therewith for the advancement of learning'. Like Oxford and Cambridge, however, the new university would award degrees only to those students who recognised the supreme authority of the king and who adhered to the Book of Common Prayer. In other words, dissenters could attend lectures but could progress no further. The new university was, after all, administered and controlled by the dean and chapter of Durham and had been established in connection with the Cathedral Church of Durham. These bodies did not intend to undermine their own foundations.

88 *The old Quaker Meeting House on Claypath.*

89 *Memorial in the cathedral to Bishop Shute Barrington.*

90 *Examination time for students at Durham University, 1842.*

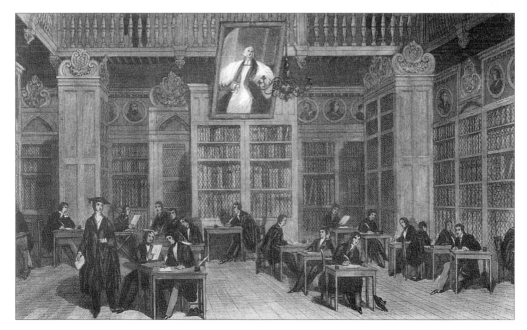

But it was never the intention of the founders of Durham University that it should be just a northern training ground for Anglican priests. The doctrines of the Church of England would be observed by the students but subjects other than divinity were to be studied, including, as one cleric put it, 'the numerous tribes of medical sciences with names terminating in -ogy'. On the other hand, it was not until 1908 that compulsory student attendance at church on Sundays was abolished and only in 1910 did the dean and chapter finally relinquish control over the university.

The Church was left to foot most of the bills for the setting up of the new university, financial help from the laity not forthcoming as had been expected. Bishop van Mildert donated Durham Castle and several thousand pounds as his contribution but on his death in 1836 funds were still needed. The old castle would itself prove to be a great drain on the university coffers. Various measures were taken to improve and consolidate the funding of the new establishment but by 1857 serious thought was being given to closing down the entire enterprise. Then finance was reorganised, new funds were found and the venture continued, although it was claimed that students at Durham had to meet expenses as heavy as those levied on their counterparts at Oxford and Cambridge.

In 1834 Newcastle-upon-Tyne, having earlier failed to secure its own university, was pacified by having the Newcastle-upon-Tyne College for Medicine in connection with the University of Durham sited there. It was not until 1870 that this college became a complete part of Durham University. Most radical of all the developments associated with the creation of Durham University was the foundation in 1837 of a School of Civil Engineering, probably the first in the land. It eventually failed because funds could not be found either to award scholarships to engineering students or to establish a chair in the subject.

University College, based in and around Durham Castle, is the oldest of the Durham colleges. Women were not admitted to University College until 1987. Hatfield College, in North Bailey and just a short distance from Palace Green, was founded in 1846 and named after the 14th-century Bishop Thomas Hatfield. The intention was to provide a residence for young men who did not have the financial resources to live in University College and the initial housing was in the elegant 18th-century *Red Lion* coaching inn. With its lower fees, Hatfield College provided a useful resource for the university, as a result of which the Archdeacon's Inn was reopened in 1851 and renamed Bishop Cosin's Hall. It remained open for just 13 years.

Although the combined college of St Bede and St Hild became a full member of the university only in 1979, ceasing at that time to be a College of Education, the two separate establishments have long and distinguished histories. The College of the Venerable Bede was founded at Durham in 1839 as a Church of England college to train young men as schoolteachers. It thus predates Hatfield College as a foundation. Its first buildings were established between 1845 and 1847, with further extensions

91   *Dunelm House.*

between then and 1858 and more in 1875. One of Durham's modern architectural gems is the beautiful Bede College chapel designed by Seely and Paget, built on the eve of the outbreak of World War II and described by Pevsner as an 'outstanding work of modern ecclesiastical architecture'. St Hild's College for intending women teachers dates from 1858. The west wing was added in 1907, the chapel in 1912 and the east wing in 1925. Both colleges had more modern buildings added in the middle of the 20th century. Bede accepted degree students for the first time in 1892 while Hild's ladies were admitted for degree in 1896, a year after the university started to grant degrees to women.

As the university grew, it accepted that not all students needed to be members of a college. Such 'unattached' students were admitted from 1871 and some formed themselves into societies. One such was St Cuthbert's Society, formed in 1888 and followed in 1899 by a hostel for women students, Abbey House, on the peninsula. In 1919 this became St Mary's College, housed since 1952 in a virtual French château on Elvet Hill. A new building was added in 1962. St Aidan's College, on Windmill Hill since 1964, was another establishment which started life as a non-collegiate group of women students. The main building was designed by Sir Basil Spence. Nestling beneath the great east end of the cathedral, St Chad's College, established in 1904, is situated in the North Bailey. A little way along the road, in the South Bailey, is St John's College, set up in 1909. Both foundations were originally for

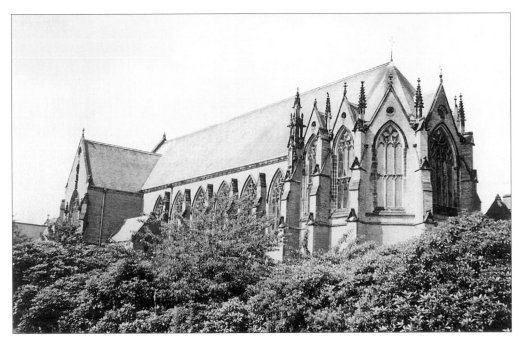

92 *Ushaw College Chapel.*

theological students and both can boast 18th-century buildings as part of their premises.

Four miles to the west of Durham City, near the village of Bearpark, is Ushaw College, a Roman Catholic seminary opened on its present site in 1808. In 1968, it was licensed as a hall of residence for Durham University. Ushaw is a most unlikely collection of buildings to be encountered in this part of the world, standing as it does on a high hilltop between the Rivers Browney and Deerness. The insides are even more amazing than the exterior. The most outstanding is the Gothic-style chapel by Pugin, whose descendants also worked at Ushaw. This seminary's history dates back to the 16th century when there was founded at Douai in France a college to train Roman Catholic missionaries who would work in England. In 1793, during the French Revolution, the college was seized by the authorities, at which point the students sought and found refuge in England. In 1794 they assembled at Tudhoe, near Spennymoor in County Durham, at the school where the eminent Yorkshire naturalist Charles Waterton was educated. Later that year they went to Crook Hall near Lanchester, a few miles to the west of Durham, and in 1808 to their new home at Ushaw, building having begun there in 1804 following the site's purchase in 1799. The college tripled in size between the 1830s and the 1930s. The list of former students of Ushaw College is impressive by any standards; among those educated here is Francis Barraud, the man who went on to create the famous dog and gramophone trademark for 'His Master's Voice'.

93   *Ushaw College.*

One of the most amusing men ever to occupy a student's room in the keep of Durham Castle was Edward, later the Rev. Edward, Bradley, better known to posterity as the author and cartoonist Cuthbert Bede. Born the son of a doctor in March 1827, he was educated first at Kidderminster Grammar School and, in 1845, admitted as a theology undergraduate of the University of Durham. On graduating in 1848, Bradley spent some time in Oxford before his ordination in 1850, after which he took up the post of Rector of Stretton, in Rutland. Using the pseudonym of 'Cuthbert Bede', borrowed from the two great saints buried in the cathedral, Bradley penned some amusing accounts of university life as it was in his day. While still an undergraduate, he drew a series of sketches which he titled 'Ye Freshmonne, his adventures at University College, Durham' in which, while spending his first night at the *Waterloo Inn*, he dreams that he has become a bishop but is rudely awakened to spend the next day in pursuit of suitable lodgings which he eventually finds in 'Ye Castle'. When Bradley later tried to sell a number of his sketches to *Punch* magazine, he was told that he needed to adapt them to represent Oxford University. Durham was unacceptable, apparently, as a backdrop. At the time of his death in 1889 he was Vicar of Grantham.

The focal point of the market place is an equestrian statue of Charles William Vane Stewart, 3rd Marquess of Londonderry, 1st Earl Vane and Baron Stewart of Stewarts Court (1778-1854), in the uniform of a hussar. He was ancestrally connected with the monarchs of Scotland. Initially a soldier and politician, the marquess became Lord Lieutenant of Durham and is remembered today as the founder of Seaham Harbour on the Durham coast. The statue, made of plaster coated with copper, an early example of electroplating, was executed by a sculptor from Milan, Raffaelle Monti. When they realised just how large the statue was to be, the City Council tried to have it erected on Palace Green instead of in their market place. They failed in their endeavour and at the unveiling on 2 December 1861 there were present units of

94   *Statue of the 3rd Marquess of Londonderry in the market place.*

the North Durham Militia, Durham City Rifle Volunteers, Sunderland Rifle Volunteers and Seaham Artillery Volunteers. The statue of the 'bold sabreur' was restored in 1952.

Despite having been a brilliant and daring soldier, friend of the great and famous of his day and doer of good deeds, the 3rd Marquess of Londonderry was not popular with Durham's miners, many of them his employees. In 1822 Stewart inherited his title, as well as the lucrative family estates in Ireland, when his half-brother the 2nd Marquess of Londonderry, Robert Stewart, Viscount Castlereagh, Foreign Secretary and Leader of the House of Commons, committed suicide. Three years earlier, the 3rd Marquess had married Frances Anne Vane-Tempest, heiress to estates in Ireland and County Durham. At the same time he changed his name to Vane.

Born in Dublin in 1778, he was educated at Eton College. When just 16, he acquired a commission in the army in MacNamara's Regiment. Just a year later, he had risen to the rank of major in the 106th Foot from which he moved, after distinguished service in the Netherlands and Germany, to the Royal Irish Dragoons. Acquiring great fame as a cavalry commander, Stewart served under Sir John Moore and the Duke of Wellington. By 1808 he led the Hussar Brigade, subsequently served as adjutant-general to Wellington and took over from the Prince Regent as Colonel of the 10th Hussars and then of the 2nd Life Guards. As a statesman, he served as British Ambassador to Vienna. After his marriage, Charles Stewart went to live a few miles north of Stockton at Wynyard Park and bought another estate, which included several collieries, at Seaham. As well as sinking new, deep, coastal mineshafts, he constructed a railway to carry his coal to Sunderland. The harbour and docks he created at Seaham Harbour had taken three years to complete when they were opened in 1831.

What alienated the 3rd Marquess from the common people of Durham was his entrenched opposition to reform of almost any sort. He would not allow his mines to be inspected, he opposed the raising of the statutory school leaving age to 12, was not in favour of the 1832 Reform Bill, did all he could to prevent the formation of mining trade unions and brought Cornish tin miners to the county to break a strike of his own colliery employees. He fought two duels during his life and was once set upon by a Durham mob. And, on 19 July 1821, the day of the coronation of the new king, George IV, the marquess had what he perceived to be his generosity thrown back, quite literally, in his face:

> In the city of Durham, a small ox, the gift of lord Stuart (now marquis of Londonderry), was roasted at the head of Old Elvet. It was soon cut in pieces, which, together with a quantity of bread, were thrown indiscriminately to the public; but no sooner was this done, than the populace immediately commenced pelting, with it, those on the platform, so that his lordship's generosity on this occasion was literally thrown away. Several barrels of ale were also given away, which added considerably to the tumult and confusion. (M.A. Richardson, *Local Historian's Table Book*, 1846)

By comparison, on the same day:

> At North Shields a quantity of meat and bread [not provided by Lord Londonderry!] was distributed to the public in a manner highly commendable. Several tables were set out in the Market-place, and a loaf of bread, and two pounds of meat on a cabbage leaf, with fourpence to purchase ale, were given to such poor persons who had procured tickets for them.

Two years later there was a dreadful explosion at Rainton Colliery, which was owned by the marquess:

> … fifty-three men and boys perished, and several others were dreadfully hurt, two of whom afterwards died; twelve horses were also killed. A little before eight o'clock, one of the overmen, and soon after, one of the workmen, descended the pit, and succeeded in bringing several of the sufferers to bank; and in the course of the morning the bodies of all who had perished were brought up, with the exception of four, who were in the most distant parts of the mine. The bodies presented a most shocking spectacle, being much burnt, and many of them very much mutilated. (M.A. Richardson, *Local Historian's Table Book*, 1846)

The marquess's wife, Lady Frances Anne, had a very different relationship with the miners. On several occasions she entertained 'upwards of 3,000 pitmen and workpeople employed on her ladyship's collieries' to festivities which included the serving of 'eight bullocks, fifteen sheep, a ton of plum pudding, a ton and a half of bread, one hundred bushels of potatoes and fifty barrels of ale'. She was also the first person to suggest the setting up of funds to provide aged miners with retirement homes, an idea which came to fruition some 40 years afterwards.

The architect of most of the present St Nicholas' church, the parish church of the city, was J.F. Pritchett of Darlington. Built between 1857 and 1858 to a neo-Gothic design and occupying the entire north side of the market place, it was the first church in the city to be adorned with a spire and was called in the national press of the time 'the most beautiful specimen of church architecture in the north of England'. Pritchett had not originally been engaged to build a completely new church. The old building had undergone extensive, often makeshift, repairs over the centuries and even suffered the ignominy of being almost hidden from view by a piazza built in front of practically the whole of its south face during the 18th century. This piazza was used subsequently as a corn market before being removed in 1854. During the first half of the 19th century, all sorts of schemes were devised and costed to continue the repairs of the old church until it was realised in 1857 that such piecemeal efforts were doing no good at all. It was finally decided that a completely new church had to be built. Generous financial assistance from the new incumbent, George Townshend Fox, and a donation of £1,000 from the Marchioness of Londonderry did much to bring about this decision. Pritchett revised his designs and added a steeple to them. When this was felt to be too expensive an addition, Mr Fox donated the required £300. The interior of St Nicholas' church today would be quite alien to Messrs Pritchett and Fox for a great deal of work had been undertaken to change it by 1981.

By the middle of the 19th century, the Guildhall had ceased to be a suitable building, nor was it large enough, to accommodate all the business transacted by the City, so in 1850 a new town hall was proposed by the then mayor, William Henderson, and built onto the rear of the old structure. Public subscription was again called for and in 1851 the Main Hall, as it is called, was opened. The London architect Philip Charles Hardwick designed it as a less complicated and smaller-scale version of Westminster Hall. The hammer beam roof is most impressive, as is the great west window which includes portrayals of the Corpus Christi procession, four bishops of Durham, the arms of several local families and a scene centred around King Edward III on horseback in Durham market place. Another stained-glass window is dedicated to the men of the Durham Light Infantry. The imposing fireplace is of Prudhoe stone. A fine collection of paintings adorns the wall of the Main Hall, many of them by Clement Burlison, an acclaimed artist whose father had been a businessman in Silver Street. When Burlison died in 1899, his bequest of paintings formed the basis for the City Art Gallery, known as the Burlison Gallery. Burlison was known for his

95 *Romanticised moonlit view of Durham Cathedral.*

high quality portrait painting and for producing excellent copies of pictures which hung in European art galleries. His work was often exhibited at London's Royal Academy. Durham's covered market was opened beneath the town hall in 1851.

The influential architect Ignatius Bonomi (1787-1870) lived in Durham for more than 40 years, some of that time in 5 North Bailey. He was of Italian stock, his father Giuseppe, also an architect, having been persuaded to leave Florence to work for the great Robert Adam in England, where he arrived in 1767 and remained apart from a brief visit to Italy in 1783-4. The family home was in London and Giuseppe Bonomi achieved moderate fame, even being mentioned by Jane Austen in *Sense and Sensibility*.

In 1803 Ignatius Bonomi joined the family business to train as an architect. His father died in 1808 and Ignatius decided to carry on the practice. In 1813, having done some work in North Yorkshire, principally at Skelton Castle, he was successful in his application to be appointed to the post of County Bridge Surveyor for Durham and Bonomi chose Durham City as his base. In 1837, aged 50, he married Charlotte Anne Fielding. The wedding took place first in an Anglican church, Charlotte Anne being the daughter of a Church of England clergyman, but they were married again a few days later in St Cuthbert's Roman Catholic church in Durham City. Bonomi was, at this time, a Roman Catholic and St Cuthbert's was one of the churches of which he had been the architect some years earlier.

Until this time, Bonomi lived in a house he had designed himself, Elvet Hill, but he and his new bride moved into 5 North Bailey which had been occupied until then by Charlotte Anne and her sister Sophy, who continued to live with them. The two ladies had run a school there. Bonomi's office was almost opposite at 45 North Bailey. He was County Bridge Surveyor for 37 years, retiring from the post in 1850 at the age of 63. He did not give up work, however, but continued with his private practice. In 1856 the Bonomis went to live in London, where Charlotte Anne died in 1860. Ignatius Bonomi died in 1870 at his Wimbledon home, 'The Camels', which he had designed himself.

The original 7 North Bailey, replaced in 1966 by a new university building, was once owned by a remarkable character called John Gully. He died at this elegant home in 1863, in his 80th year, having moved into the city because of his frailty. His later life and his vast circle of influential friends gives no hint of his modest beginning. Before the end of his first year in business the young Gully had been languishing in gaol, imprisoned for debt. The story of how he rose from bankruptcy and obscurity to become a Member of Parliament as well as an exceedingly wealthy colliery owner and keeper of fine racehorses reads almost like a fairy tale.

John Gully was born in 1783 at Wick in Gloucestershire where his parents kept the *Rose and Crown Inn*. While he was still young, the family moved to Bristol where his father traded as a butcher until his death, which occurred before John had attained his majority. Mrs Gully carried on the business until her son was 21 when she handed it over to him. It was soon obvious to the young man that she had not been a good businesswoman and that her books did not balance. For his mother's ineptitude, John Gully was convicted of debt and consigned to the King's Bench Prison. Here he found he had plenty of time to exercise for, as well as plying his trade as a butcher before awaiting His Majesty's pleasure, he had begun to find considerable local fame as a pugilist or bare-knuckle boxer. Word of Gully's imprisonment soon reached the ears of England's champion boxer, the 'Game Chicken', Henry Pearce, who visited him in gaol. In the afternoon a bout was arranged between them. It was a good-humoured affair but both men threw some heavy punches, Gully having no need to be ashamed of his performance. He felt that, given time and training, he would be able to beat Pearce. A patron of boxing named Fletcher Reid heard about the prison bout and wanted to see the two men meet properly in the prize ring. He paid off Gully's debts and sent him to Virginia Water to be trained.

Although John Gully was almost six feet tall and of an athletic build, he did not look like a typical boxer. His greatest strengths were his courage and confidence in his ability. The fight with Pearce eventually took place at Hailsham in Sussex in October 1805. Some of the greatest patrons of the sport were present that day, including the Duke of Clarence, later King William IV. After 64 rounds of a fight which lasted for one hour 17 minutes, Gully conceded defeat, but Pearce admitted that it was the hardest fight he had ever had. When he retired from the ring, Pearce handed over his title to John Gully. It was two years before any challenger for the title came forward: Gully's opponent was a Mr Gregson and the fight went to 36 rounds. At the end of this, both men, not surprisingly, had difficulty standing. One beating by Gully should have been enough for any man but six months later Gregson came back for more. This time, in May 1808, it took the champion just 28 rounds to defeat him. The crowd which turned up to see this bout was enormous, quite remarkable considering that the fight was supposed to be a secret. Having suggested to Gregson that he should retire from the ring, Gully climbed into Lord Barrymore's carriage and was driven to the tavern he owned by then in Carey Street in London's Lincoln's Inn Fields.

Soon afterwards, Gully himself retired from boxing and for the next few years devoted his time to tavern-keeping. He did, nevertheless, find time to cultivate a much more lucrative interest. He loved horse-racing and was either clever or lucky with the bets he placed because he made so much money through gambling that he soon had enough to buy Hare Park in Hertfordshire and then Ackworth Park in Yorkshire. Here he mixed with the gentry. Gully had made his mark, was making money and was enjoying life to the full as a country landowner. He had come a long way from debtors' prison.

John Gully was intelligent, good-humoured and kind and was readily accepted by his new friends. He never tried to hide his past but answered honestly questions about his early life. He continued to pursue his racing interests and kept permanent lodgings at Newmarket. Soon his reputation as a racehorse breeder and proprietor brought him to the notice of one of the foremost betting men in the land, His Royal Highness The Prince Regent, later King George IV. Gully became his racing adviser and continued to breed some of the finest racehorses of the time. His horses won the Derby three times along with the Oaks, the St Leger and the Two Thousand Guineas. On two famous occasions he lost £40,000 and £85,000 but later recouped these losses. In 1854 his net winnings were just short of £11,000, a phenomenal sum for those days.

In 1832 Gully was elected Member of Parliament for Pontefract, which he represented as a Liberal. His time in the House of Commons was devoted largely to supporting the campaign which sought to curb wasteful public expenditure. His speeches were neither many nor brilliant but what he did say was timely and sensible. The most peculiar aspect of Gully's time at Westminster was that he had never had any ambition to be there: he had stood for election merely to win a bet!

Apart from his skills as a prize-fighter and breeder of superb racehorses, John Gully is best remembered as a colliery-owner. He gradually withdrew from his gambling pursuits and so avoided the bankruptcy which befell so many of his friends. The lilac coat he always wore on the racecourse was seen less and less as he invested

96   *Threshing time in Durham, early 20th century.*

97   *Farm near Hallgarth Street, late 19th century.*

98   *The building of North Road railway viaduct.*

more of his time in land and coal-mines in the north of England. He bought shares in the Hetton Coal Company at a time when geologists were saying that to attempt to work any of the projected seams would be crass folly. The geologists were wrong and Gully hung on to his shares, watching as they increased in value. Next he joined forces with Sir William Chaytor and together they financed the sinking of collieries at Thornley. He also had a large interest in the Trimdon collieries but in 1862 sold his shares in them to buy the Wingate Grange estate along with its collieries and these Gully retained until his death. Just before his purchase of Wingate he was living in Hampshire, but he then moved to Cocken Hall near Durham. He was buried, however, near one of his former homes, close to Pontefract. Gully married twice and fathered 24 children.

Robert Surtees of Mainsforth was born in the city's South Bailey on 1 April 1779. When his father died in 1802, he forsook the legal profession, for which he had been prepared at Oxford University, and retired to Mainsforth. After marrying in 1807, he settled down to write his monumental history of the county of Durham, the first volume of which was published in 1816, the second in 1820, the third in 1823 and the fourth, posthumously, in 1840. Robert Surtees was buried on 15 February 1834 at Bishop Middleham. Two months later a meeting in Durham decided to honour and to perpetuate Surtees' memory:

> April 27. A meeting was held at the *Queen's Head* inn, Durham, John Ralph Fenwick, esq., M.D., in the chair, when it was determined to establish a literary society, to be called 'The Surtees Society' in honour of the late Robert Surtees, of Mainsforth, esq., the historian of Durham, and in accordance with his taste and pursuits, to have for its object the publication of unedited MSS. illustrative of the intellectual, the moral, the religious, and the social condition of those parts of England and Scotland,

99   *Elvet railway station.*

included on the east between the Humber and the Firth of Forth, and on the west between the Mersey and the Clyde, a region which at one period constituted the ancient kingdom of Northumberland. (M.A. Richardson, *Local Historian's Table Book*, 1846)

Also in 1834, on 18 June, a regatta took place on the River Wear.

At six o'clock on the evening, the different boats upon the river Wear, proceeded in grand procession from the Prebend's bridge up the river to Old Durham, accompanied by a band of music, which played the greater part of the way. The rowers in the several boats were all dressed in their different uniforms, and each boat had a small flag flying from its stern. The boats afterwards came back to the Prebend's bridge, and each took in some ladies, and proceeded up the water again towards Old Durham. The rowing on the water terminated a little after nine o'clock; after which, a quantity of fireworks were set off from a platform, erected for that purpose at the water side, near the Banks mill. On the following day, a similar exhibition took place. (M.A. Richardson, *Local Historian's Table Book*, 1846)

By the middle of the 19th century, Durham City was served by several railway companies. The top of Durham's North Road, a thoroughfare completed in 1831, is dominated by the enormous railway viaduct. With 11 arches and standing almost 30 metres high, it dates from 1857. One of the best views of the cathedral, indeed of the whole city, is to be had by rail passengers crossing this structure. The viaduct carries the railway to Durham's station, set high to the north-west of the city and also built in 1857. The first railway station, built by the Durham and Sunderland Railway in 1839, was in the nearby village of Shincliffe. It operated until 1893, in which year Elvet station opened at the head of Old Elvet and was in use until 1931. The Magistrates' Courts were built on the site when it was demolished in 1963. In 1844 a station designed by G.T. Andrews was opened in Gilesgate, a spur connecting that point with the London to Newcastle line at Belmont Junction. In 1857 this became a goods-only station, eventually closing in 1966.

101   *The piper, Jamie Allan.*

The House of Correction, under Elvet Bridge, was the last home of a character once as famous throughout the country as Robin Hood. He was Jamie Allan, a celebrated Northumbrian piper and sometime villain. It is said that his is one of the ghosts which haunts Durham, the strains of his pipes still being heard around Elvet Bridge. Jamie Allan, sometimes known as Jemmy or Jimmy, was a gypsy born in about 1734 near Rothbury in Northumberland. His story is a remarkable one, as recalled at the time of his death:

> 13th November, 1810. Died in the House of Correction at Durham, where he had been confined upwards of seven years, under sentence of transportation for life, James Allan, a character well-known in most parts of the United Kingdom, particularly in Northumberland, where he was known by the name of Jemmy, the duke's piper, and was in early life a great proficient on the pipes. He was capitally convicted of horse-stealing, at the assizes held in Durham, in 1803, and received sentence of death, but was afterwards pardoned on condition of transportation for life; but on account of his age and infirmities, his sentence could not be carried into execution. He had nearly completed his 77th year, and, for the greatest part of his confinement, was afflicted with a complication of disorders. Had the chequered life of this notorious character been prolonged a little, he would have regained his liberty, as the first signature of the Prince Regent, officially addressed to the city of Durham, was a free pardon for Allan; but death had removed him beyond the reach of royal clemency. (M.A. Richardson, *Local Historian's Table Book*, 1846)

Many adventures are ascribed to Allan but few can be verified and he is always regarded as a romantic figure despite his obvious faults and shortcomings. He is said to have played his pipes before royalty, was married at least three times, once bigamously, and frequently enlisted in and deserted from the army. There is no apparent explanation of why the Prince Regent was so ready to pardon him. James Allan was youngest-but-one of a family of six. Taking up the pipes at the age of 14, he learned quickly from his father. He possessed 'an accurate ear, a refined taste and great sensibility to the beauties of harmony'. He was remarkably adroit at learning a new tune and was admired for the exquisite expression of feeling and simplicity which distinguished his performances. His biographer in 1828 records that he 'could play on the highland bagpipe but he excelled most on the sweet small pipes. He also played well on the Northumberland raising or gathering pipes, called the "great pipes" to distinguish them from the small ones; and could perform very well on the Union pipes.'

Allan was summoned to play to the Countess of Northumberland and was, according to some sources, made her piper. She gave him, when he left her service, a 'pair of small pipes she had procured from Edinburgh, handsomely-made of ivory and decorated with silver chains'. He was given a second set of pipes by the next Duchess of Northumberland. Allan was interred in St Nicholas' churchyard, Durham, although he had asked to be buried at Rothbury. His pipes he left to 'two gentlemen of North Shields', the port where he spent his winters when he was a free man. A few verses were written about Jamie Allan soon after his death:

> All ye whom Music's charms inspire
> Who skilful minstrels do admire.
> All ye whom bagpipe lilts can fire
> 'Tween Wear and Tweed,
> Come, strike with me, the mournful lyre,
> For ALLAN'S dead.
>
> No more where Coquet's stream doth glide
> Shall we view JEMMY in his pride,
> With bagpipe buckled to his side,
> And nymphs and swains
> In groups collect, at even-tide,
> To hear his strains.
>
> When elbow moved, and bellows blew,
> On green or floor the dancers flew,
> In many turns ran through and through
> With cap'ring canter,
> And aye their nimble feet beat true
> To his sweet chanter.

The fine *Royal County Hotel* across Elvet Bridge is a hostelry with a fascinating history. The present establishment is made up of several buildings of varying dates and the property seen today was formerly 57-60 Old Elvet along with the now-vanished Chapel Passage. The famous balcony across the central frontage of the hotel was created in two parts, the stone balustrade early in the 19th century, the ironwork in the late 19th century. For a short time in the late 18th century, part of the building was used as a boarding school. The original properties on this site, now much

102   *The* Royal County Hotel *in Old Elvet, late 19th century.*

changed, date from *c.*1630. One was the home of Lady Mary Radcliffe, a member or the famous Roman Catholic Derwentwater family of Dilston Castle. Her half-sister was Lady Mary Tudor, natural daughter to King Charles II. Another of the houses was occupied by Elizabeth Bowes, aunt to the Earl of Strathmore's wife, Mary Eleanor Bowes. It was she who inherited the vast properties of the Bowes family but her father's will insisted that her husband had to take her family name. So it was that John Lyon, Earl of Strathmore, took the name of Bowes, even though an Act of Parliament was required to enable this to happen.

One of the peculiarities of this site is that for a long time there were two neighbouring hostelries both known as the *Waterloo* and named after the great British victory of 1815. The now-demolished *Waterloo Hotel*, formerly 61 Old Elvet, appears to have been known in its earliest days as the *Green Dragon Inn*. It is difficult to ascertain when either property first became a hostelry although it is certain that the present *Royal County* was known as the *Waterloo Hotel* in 1820, for in that year the owner, William Ward, was advertising his premises in a local gazetteer. Presumably the name Waterloo was taken soon after the battle, such was national pride in the victory. By 1827, Ward's hotel was advertised as the *Waterloo Hotel and Posting House*. In 1834 the property had passed to Elizabeth Ward and was again known simply as the *Waterloo Hotel*. By 1846, no. 61 was also advertising itself as the *Waterloo Hotel*, run by John Thwaites, victualler; in 1827, he had run the *Queen's Head Inn and Posting House* in the North Bailey, which he administered until moving to the *Waterloo*. On old maps, the two Old Elvet properties are distinctly shown as *Ward's Waterloo Hotel* and *Thwaites' Waterloo Hotel*. Elizabeth Ward was succeeded by the Ward brothers in 1850 but in 1851 the place was run by W. Thomas Ward. Strangely enough, in 1850 both properties seem to have been called the *Waterloo Hotel and Commercial Inn* but in 1864 there was a change. The Thwaites' property, no. 61, became the *Waterloo Inn* while no. 60 passed from the ownership of the Wards to Thomas Turner, formerly an hotelier in Darlington, and changed its name to the *County Hotel*. In 1866 the Thwaites gave up the *Waterloo*, which was taken over by A. Millar, while the *County* passed into the hands of Mrs Turner. Thereafter, while the *Waterloo Hotel* changed hands fairly frequently, the *County*, owned by Mrs Turner until 1871, was then run by Mrs White until well into the 1880s. Sometime before 1900, after a visit by Albert, Prince of Wales (soon to become King Edward VII), the *County* became the *Royal County*

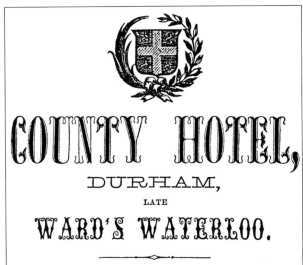

103   *Victorian advertisement for the* County Hotel.

104   *The Reverend John Bacchus Dykes.*

Hotel and was administered by a progression of manageresses. How the post office managed to discern which Waterloo was which in the early days of the hotels may never be known!

The former Chapel Passage used to cross what is now the car park of the *Royal County Hotel* and led to the Methodist chapel, opened in 1808 and demolished in 1968. Beside it was a three-storey house for the preacher. This was the second Methodist chapel in the city, an earlier one, probably simply a converted dwelling house, having existed in Court Lane.

No. 34 Old Elvet was once the home of one of the greatest Victorian writers of hymn tunes, John Bacchus Dykes, at one time minor canon and precentor of Durham Cathedral. He resigned as precentor to become vicar of nearby St Oswald's church from 1862-74. At the age of 12, Dykes had been appointed assistant organist at St John's church, Hull where his grandfather was the incumbent. After studying first in Wakefield, he moved on to St Catherine's Hall, Cambridge where he read for a classics degree and became president of the Cambridge University Musical Society. As well as the organ, he also played the piano, violin and horn. When *Hymns Ancient and Modern* was being mooted, Dykes heard about the new collection and offered some of his tunes to its music editor, Dr Monk. Seven of them, including 'Melita', to which 'Eternal Father, Strong to Save' is almost always sung, were included in the first edition with 24 more appearing in subsequent editions. Altogether Dykes composed over 300 hymn tunes, possibly best remembered being those for 'Nearer My God to Thee', 'Holy, Holy, Holy! Lord God Almighty', 'Jesu, Lover of My Soul', 'Lead, Kindly Light', 'Praise to the Holiest in the Height', 'Ride On! Ride On In Majesty' and 'The King of Love My Shepherd Is'. For his high church views, John Bacchus Dykes found himself at odds with authority. So large was the Durham parish of St Oswald's that he needed two curates as assistants. The bishop, however, would not entertain these appointments unless Dykes gave him an undertaking that they would not use incense, would not turn their backs on the congregation while involved in the service of Holy Communion and would not wear coloured stoles. Dykes refused to agree to these conditions with the result that he became severely overworked and died aged just fifty-three. He lies buried in the churchyard extension of St Oswald's.

Across the road from the Magistrates Courts in Old Elvet is the new part of Durham Prison while a short way across the green, at the end of Court Lane, are the original Durham Prison and the Old Assize Courts or Crown Courts. Much controversy surrounded the building of these. Begun in 1809, their first architect, Francis Sandys, was dismissed. He was followed by George Moneypenny and then by Ignatius Bonomi who completed the project to his own plan between 1815-19. It was enlarged in 1850. Old Elvet was felt to have been spoiled by the building of the Shire Hall and the Methodist church between 1895 and 1903. Nevertheless, it is still a wide and attractive thoroughfare with some beautiful architecture.

Twelve

MINERS, CARPETS AND ORGANS

Today's city is known for its university, for a famous company of organ builders, for its county regiment, for its world-famous carpets and for its annual miners' gala. Few realise that the city had coal-mines so close to it that several were contained within its very boroughs and that in 1915 the new Durham Miners' Hall was opened at Redhills, replacing a predecessor on North Road. Many people know from personal experience or from television pictures the *Royal County Hotel*'s famous balcony on which prominent Labour Party and mineworkers' leaders have stood over the years to watch the parade of bands and lodge banners of the Durham coal-mines on Gala Day, better known locally as 'Durham Big Meeting'. The event is but a shadow of its former self since the coal-mines are now no more but for decades, on the third Saturday in July, 'The Big Meeting' was the focal point for every miner and his family.

The miners and associated trade unions meet on Smiddyhaughs, the fields which were the city's racecourse from 1733-1887, but for many of the thousands who attended every year this riverside gathering place was not always the ultimate venue. Many of the miners and their families also paraded to Palace Green and on to a service in the cathedral. The first Durham Miners' Gala was held not on the racecourse but in Wharton Park on 2 August 1871, just two years after the Durham Miners' Association itself was founded. At its height, the event was the largest annual demonstration by the working classes anywhere in the country. Just before the First World War, the crowds were often in excess of 100,000 people. At times even the colliery owners were allowed to take part in the proceedings. There were no meetings during the First World War but in 1925, the year before the General Strike, some of the Durham miners marked their gala by throwing the Dean of Durham into the River Wear. They mistook him for the Bishop of Durham, who had expressed the view that miners did not deserve an increase in pay. They carried banners proclaiming, 'To Hell with Bishops and Deans. We demand a living wage'.

After the Second World War, during which the Gala was again suspended, so many people began to attend the gathering that the racecourse was equipped with two platforms for the speakers. The great names of the Labour Party appeared on these stages and on the *Royal County Hotel*'s balcony. Clement Attlee, Stafford Cripps,

105   *Emblem of the Durham Light Infantry.*

Herbert Morrison, Ernest Bevin, Aneurin Bevan, Harold Wilson, Michael Foot and Tony Benn all came in recognition of the importance of the event to the Labour Movement at the time. It now relies for its survival on the support of more than just miners and their families but that survival, in one form or another, does seem to be assured.

Although coal was mined in the area in the Middle Ages, there is no way of knowing precisely when such activity began. The 19th century saw the sinking of hundreds of mineshafts with some of the resultant collieries more successful than others. Many of the mines in close proximity to Durham City had gone by the 1950s, closed for a variety of reasons including economic viability, although Bearpark was worked until 1984. The other colliery classified as being in Bearpark was Broom Park. Belmont had the Adelaide Pit and Broomside Colliery, while its Grange Colliery operated from 1844 until 1948. Closer to the city, Kepier Colliery was in operation before 1818, Houghall began in 1841 and Old Durham followed in 1849. Those which closed in 1924 included Brasside, Dryburn Grange, Durham Main, Kepier Grange, opened in 1844, and Framwellgate Moor, which had been in operation for six years longer. Shincliffe Colliery lasted only from 1839 to 1875 while Frankland, opened in 1840, ceased producing coal in the 1860s. Aykley Heads fared better than many, lasting from the 1880s until 1949. Also near to the city were the Florence Pit, from 1872, and the Lord Ernest Pit. Elvet Colliery was where the university library on Stockton Road now stands.

Over the years, there were hundreds of mining accidents, many of them close to Durham City itself. Mining could be a dangerous occupation. At Dryburn Grange Colliery in 1863 Solomon Halliday, a hewer aged 27, was killed by a fall of stone. In 1864 George Cole, an onsetter aged 54, was crushed by the descending cage. 1866 saw the life of James Hughes, aged 14, taken when he was crushed by tubs and in 1867 the 57-year-old John Trippet was killed by a fall of coal. Other causes of miners' deaths included being run over by trucks, falling down a shaft, being crushed by machinery, caught in an explosion of gas and being pulled onto a rope drum by the rope. Many miners also died, while at work, 'of natural causes' as the reports put it but many of the complaints were almost certainly related to their occupation and to their working conditions.

106 *Bottom of the pit shaft.*

Many miners were included among the men who served, particularly in the two world wars, in the county's own regiment, which today has its own museum, opened in 1969 at Aykley Heads, as well as a memorial chapel in the cathedral. The Durham Light Infantry, usually known as the D.L.I., originated in 1758 when the 68th Regiment of Foot was raised by General John Lambton. Half a century later, as a new light infantry regiment, it was despatched to be part of the Duke of Wellington's army fighting in Spain and Portugal. Subsequently, during service in the Crimea and New Zealand, three members of the regiment were awarded Victoria Crosses.

After 1881, and renamed the Durham Light Infantry, the regiment fought in Egypt and South Africa. By the end of the First World War, the D.L.I. had raised 43 batallions, had been involved in all of the great battles and had been awarded six more V.Cs. During the Second World War, nine battalions were raised and fought with distinction. After the war, the regiment's size was gradually reduced, leaving eventually only the 1st Battalion. In 1968, the D.L.I. was merged with three other infantry regiments to form The Light Infantry and, on 12 December, paraded its colours for the final time in Durham Cathedral.

The opposite bank of the Wear from the D.L.I. Museum used to accommodate the Mackay Carpet Factory, a concern which has now moved to premises not far out of Durham City. Cloth was certainly woven in Durham as early as 1243 and in the years that followed the Guild of Weavers was active in many ways, not least in attempting on several occasions to establish training facilities for young men, and eventually for young girls, to learn the trade. Not all of these ventures were successful, in fact some were abject failures, with evidence that the teachers were defrauding those who had provided their funds. By 1737, however, John Starforth, 'weaver and manufacturer', was awarded a loan of £392 14s. od. 'to develop woollen manufacture in Durham City'. By 1774 Starforth was employing 'some hundreds of persons'.

107 *Broomside Colliery near Durham in the late 19th century.*

During the 1790s he had 700 weavers and was concentrating his efforts on woollen and carpet cloth. By 1801 Starforth's woollen and carpet factory was easily the largest industry in the city. He employed more than 800 workers, over one tenth of the population. Then, in 1805, the business went bankrupt. Several abortive efforts were made to restart weaving in the city and in 1814 Gilbert Henderson was loaned some £400 to fund his attempt. He was of Scottish descent and had been employed in the Starforth company; indeed it was he who wound up the company after its failure.

At the age of 26, after a serious illness, Henderson had been an invalid, able to move at first only in a wheelchair and then on sticks. He lived in the village of Kirk Merrington, near Spennymoor, where he befriended the local weavers and learned all aspects of their craft. In 1810 he opened a factory in the village to weave carpets. Within three years he was employing 60 people there. Taking 30 of these employees with him, in 1813 he transferred production to Durham City where there already existed the carpet factory of Gainforth and Blackett. His business flourished despite the workers being involved in a long strike in 1819. In order to produce Brussels carpets, he brought what were known as Brussels looms to the city, all but smuggled out of Kidderminster. In 1824 there was a disastrous fire at the factory and in the same year, at the age of 42, Gilbert Henderson died. His wife Ann took over the running of the business while his elder son, John, then aged 17, was still serving his time in the factory learning every aspect of carpet production. In 1828 John Henderson began to run the firm. The business continued to expand and prosper and in 1835 his brother William joined him. John Henderson was elected Liberal Member 1849 and is remembered for his part in the building of the city's new town hall.

In 1854 steam power was introduced to work the looms but handlooms still continued to be used. By exhibiting its wares at the Great Exhibition of 1851, the company found even wider fame. Eventually both John and William withdrew from active management and John's sons attempted to take up the reins, Arthur Henderson proving himself the most interested. The Henderson Carpet Factory continued in production until 1903 when it was sold to Crossley's and almost the entire workforce made redundant.

In 1861, at the age of 12, a boy called Hugh Mackay had begun to work for Henderson's in the weaving shed. By 1880 he was works manager. When Henderson's sold out to Crossley's, Hugh Mackay leased some buildings and machinery not sold to them in order to begin carpet manufacture in his own right. He took on men and women who had worked for Henderson's. It was not long before the 16 looms originally leased from Henderson's were unable to keep up with demand. They were not, in any case, really suitable for the carpet types being produced. Before 1914, Mackay's were producing some of the highest-quality carpets in Britain, one with a pile two centimetres deep.

Following Hugh Mackay's death in 1924, his son Laurence took over the business, known since 1921 as Hugh Mackay & Co. Ltd. By 1929, 125 people were employed by the company. In the 1950s John Mackay joined his father as Joint Managing Director. Laurence Mackay died in 1966. Mackays have undertaken dozens of special commissions, one of the most interesting being at the Meeting House in Philadelphia U.S.A. Having been provided with little more than a scrap of the carpet which was in use there at the time of the signing of the Declaration of Independence in 1777, Mackay's reproduced the original carpet, perfect in every way in colour and design. In 1969 a terrible fire, started by an arsonist, severely damaged the factory. In 1980 the company's shareholders agreed that the business should be moved to land bought in 1957 by Laurence Mackay at Dragonville, just over a mile outside Durham City. There it flourished before moving again to a site to the west of Durham. Durham carpets continue today to be among the finest in the world.

A property in Durham's Hawthorn Terrace was home for more than a century to a company of superb craftsmen, ranked among the most famous organ-builders in Britain, and nowadays the largest, Harrison and Harrison. The company was founded by Thomas Harrison, already an experienced organ-builder at the age of 22 when in 1861 he started his own firm in Rochdale. His work, of the highest quality from the very start, soon commended him to the world of music. Among his early advocates was the clergyman John Bacchus Dykes of Durham who was instrumental in persuading him and his brother James to transfer their business to the City of Durham in 1872.

108 *The* Prince Bishop *river cruiser near Baths Bridge.*

The old paper-mill, which they bought and enlarged at that time, was the building in which the business was housed until late in the 20th century. As the 19th century closed, Thomas Harrison was succeeded by his sons Arthur and Harry. Under their direction the company's work included the cathedral organs of Wells, Ely, Newcastle, Ripon, Manchester, Gloucester, Worcester, Exeter, Winchester and Durham itself. To this list must be added London's Royal Albert Hall, Westminster Abbey, Westminster Cathedral, Southwark, Peterborough, Salisbury, York Minster and Magdalen College, Oxford along with Trinity, St John's and King's College, Cambridge. Harrison and Harrison organs have also been sent to most parts of the world.

Harry's son, Cuthbert Temple Lane Harrison (1905-91), left his own indelible mark on the craft of English organ-building. Educated at Durham School and Exeter College, Oxford, he entered the family business in 1927 but left for a time two years later. He joined the Royal Tank Corps and served in India from 1929-37. Then his uncle died and he returned to the company. On the outbreak of the Second World War, he became Major Harrison, Royal Artillery. Organ-building had, in any case, almost ceased during the hostilities. In 1945 he returned to Durham and it was not long before he became involved in what was quite a controversial project, the building of an organ for the new Royal Festival Hall. Three companies including Harrison and Harrison were invited to tender for the contract to build this instrument in time for the 1951 Festival of Britain. Realising the importance of this commission, Harrison's withdrew from the competition, refusing to be compromised on the issue of speed over quality. The other companies were also unable to meet the deadline and so the terms of the tender were altered. Harrison's was awarded the contract and Cuthbert Harrison worked with Ralph Downes to produce a most remarkable instrument. In 1962 Coventry Cathedral organ was another formidable Harrison and Harrison achievement.

Cuthbert Harrison became a great advocate of export, not only of organs but of craftsmen to restore and service them. He broke into the difficult North American market with considerable success and also won contracts in the Far East. He was, though, quintessentially a Durham man, lover of the county, city and, especially, the cathedral. For 40 years he was Secretary to the Friends of Durham Cathedral and he was also a founder member of the Organs Advisory Committee of the Council for the Care of Churches. Harrison was awarded the M.B.E. in 1980. The great tradition of which he was such an integral part is still perpetuated by the company and its craftsmen today.

Throughout the 20th century, Durham City has gradually been changed. One of the most radical changes was in 1909, when Durham County Council, with its red-brick Shire Hall headquarters built in the city's Old Elvet between 1895-8, became the first in the country to be Labour controlled. In 1963, when the county council moved to its new County Hall at Aykley Heads, 'Old Shire Hall', as it was known, became the administrative centre for Durham University. The building has much to recommend it. Its copper-coloured dome is something of a landmark. Its entrance hall is tiled to a degree which fascinates the visitor and the council chamber is acoustically superb. There is a great deal of Weardale marble in its make-up along with stained glass from Glasgow and woodwork from Newcastle.

Many of the Durham colleges are post-Second World War and have been established to the south of the city. The first of these was Grey College, built on Fountains Field, whose first students were admitted in 1959. It was named after the great parliamentary reformer, the second Earl Grey. Taking its name from one of the university's founders is Van Mildert College, which admitted its first students in 1965 while nearby Trevelyan College opened its doors in 1967. Named after the famous historian G.M. Trevelyan, a former chancellor of the university, in 1969 it won a Civic Trust Award. Collingwood College, the first in Durham to be conceived and constructed as a fully co-educational residential college, dates from 1972 and takes its name from the distinguished Cambridge mathematician Sir Edward Collingwood, a former Chairman of the Council of the University of Durham. The architects were Richard Sheppard, Robson and Partners. Facilities for graduate students are catered for in various parts of the university but especially by what used

to be called the Graduate Society, founded in 1965, and subsequently renamed Ustinov College after Sir Peter Ustinov.

Most of the city centre today is largely pedestrianised. Despite misgivings by many people at various times, the changes which have been implemented have been essentially for the better, have opened up views, removed the noise, inconvenience and pollution caused by traffic and have not overly detracted from the city's intrinsic charm. Peace and calm are still to be found readily only a few minutes away from the bustling streets. Silver Street and Saddler Street were never intended for 20th-century traffic; in fact it is doubtful if passage for vehicles has ever been easy here. However, such narrow streets must have been very much a hindrance to those invading the city in days gone by.

109 *Old Shire Hall, Old Elvet.*

110 *The second Baths Bridge.*

111   *The modern Baths Bridge.*

112   *The building of Kingsgate Bridge.*

113   *Framwellgate Bridge with the Millburngate Centre beyond.*

114   *The cathedral's Millennium Window by Joseph Nuttgens.*

In 1962 a new Baths Bridge was opened, replacing the iron bridge of 1898 which had itself been a significant improvement on the wooden one constructed in 1855. Another new footbridge dating from 1962 was Kingsgate Bridge, designed by Ove Arup and Partners and linking the North Bailey, via Bow Lane, with New Elvet. But these were not the only 20th-century initiatives to assist pedestrian and vehicle movement in different parts of the city. One of the most innovative, destined to last for quarter of the century, appeared in the market place in 1932. This was Durham's world-famous, dome-topped police box, in which sat a solitary officer charged with controlling the traffic that entered the market place via Silver Street, Saddler Street, Elvet and Claypath – no easy task. The degree of congestion with which he had to deal is inconceivable to those who know the city only as it is today, with the Claypath under-pass along with the Milburngate and New Elvet bridges. In those

115 *Durham's new Gala Theatre complex.*

pre-war days the policeman could see only the Claypath traffic and had to assess for himself, from personal experience, what was waiting to enter 'his' market place from the other three directions. Motorists approaching his box devised the most peculiar, non-Highway Code hand signals to indicate their driving intentions. A driver who had ascended Silver Street and wanted to drive up Saddler Street would sometimes hold out his right arm, then wave his hand around animatedly in a circular motion and conclude by holding up two fingers, reversed.

The policeman always understood and, while to the outsider it was a crazy system, it worked. In December 1957 a new police box was equipped with two monitors linked to cameras on tall poles to help its custodian make the traffic flow more freely. This system was in operation until the end of 1975. One of the most pleasant aspects of the 43 years during which this apparently unique system operated was that whenever a tourist waved at the duty policeman or even braved the traffic to have his or her photograph taken beside the box, he or she was invariably rewarded with a smile, as were the countless motorists who had not the first idea of where they were going nor what, precisely, they were trying to do. At such times, a policeman's lot might not always have been a happy one but that smile, or grimace, gave the lie to his actual feelings!

At the beginning of the 21st century, another new traffic-calming measure, a toll or pay-to-enter scheme, was introduced to motorists wishing to negotiate Durham's market place to travel up Saddler Street. While not initially popular, it had the desired effect of continuing to reduce the traffic level in the city centre. Much earlier, in October 1960, Durham City and Durham County Councils had suggested ways in which they believed the city's traffic problems might be not simply improved but cured. Two new road bridges, Millburngate and New Elvet, would need to be constructed and several new roads would have to be built, necessitating the demolition

116   *Durham's world-famous, dome-topped police box. (Photograph courtesy of North of England Newspapers.)*

of more than 150 houses and about 40 business premises. It was projected that the entire operation would take some four years and cost between £3 and £4 million. In 1967 the new Millburngate Bridge opened to traffic, followed by the New Elvet Bridge in 1976. The building of this thoroughfare had required the demolition of the *Waterloo Hotel*.

The creation of Millburngate Bridge necessitated widespread changes to Millburngate and Framwellgate, the Old Borough. Millburngate disappeared completely, its place being taken in 1976 by the new Millburngate Shopping Centre which was later featured on a postage stamp. Before the 17th century wealthy merchants and manufacturers had made their homes here, but by the earliest years of the 19th century it was regarded as truly a slum with which few people wished to be associated and in the 1930s all the houses there, including two 16th-century cottages, were taken down. Even the council houses in Framwellgate were demolished in the 1960s.

Durham Castle and Cathedral were justifiably named a UNESCO World Heritage Site in 1987 and in 1999 the Prince Bishops shopping area linking Saddler Street to the north end of the market place was opened. To mark the millennium, the new Clayport city library and Gala Theatre were created on opposite sides of an open square.

The city visitors and residents know today saw many changes during the 20th century, almost all of them for the better. Durham is not afraid to make necessary improvements to its facilities as long as these do not detract in any way from its ageless charm.

Appendix

THE BISHOPS OF DURHAM

William Senhouse 1502-1505
Christopher Bainbridge 1507-1508
Thomas Ruthall 1509-1522
Thomas Wolsey 1522-1528
Cuthbert Tunstall (deposed, then restored) 1530-1559
James Pilkington 1561-1576
Richard Barnes 1577-1587
Matthew Hutton 1589-1595
Tobias Matthew 1595-1606
William James 1606-1617
Richard Neile 1617-1628
George Monteigne 1628-
John Howson 1628-1632
Thomas Morton 1632-1659
John Cosin 1660-1672
Nathaniel, Lord Crewe 1674-1721
William Talbot 1721-1730
Edward Chandler 1730-1750
Joseph Butler 1750-1752
Richard Trevor 1752-1771
John Egerton 1771-1787
Thomas Thurlow 1787-1791
Shute Barrington 1791-1826
William Van Mildert 1826-1836
Edward Maltby 1836-1856
Charles Thomas Longley 1857-1860
Henry Montague Villiers 1860-1861
Charles Baring 1861-1879
Joseph Barber Lightfoot 1879-1889
Brooke Foss Westcott 1890-1901
Handley Carr Glyn Moule 1901-1920
Herbert Hensley Henson 1920-1939
Alwyn Terrell Petre Williams 1939-1952
Arthur Michael Ramsey 1952-1956
Maurice Henry Harland 1956-1966
Ian Thomas Ramsey 1966-1972
John Stapylton Habgood 1973-1983
David Edward Jenkins 1984-1994
Michael Turnbull 1994-2003
Thomas Wright 2003-

Select Bibliography

Bythell, D., *Durham Castle, University College, Durham* (Jarrold & Sons Ltd., Norwich, 1985)

Clack, P., *The Book of Durham City*, (Barracuda, 1985)

Colgrave, B., *St Margaret's Church, Durham* (British Publishing Co., Gloucester, 1950)

Colgrave, B. and Gibby, C. W., *A Short Tour of Durham* (University Bookshop, S.P.C.K., Durham, 1984)

Cook, G.H., *The Story of Durham Cathedral* (Phoenix House Ltd., 1951)

Crosby, J.H., *Durham in Old Photographs* (Alan Sutton, Stroud, 1990)

Crosby, J.H., *Ignatius Bonomi of Durham, Architect* (City of Durham Trust, 1987)

Durham Photographic Society, *Then & Now – Durham* (Tempus Publishing 1999)

Eden, Sir Timothy, *Durham, The County Books series* (Robert Hale, 1952)

Gibby, C.W., *A Short History of Durham* (Cherrett Brothers, 1975)

Gillam, J.P. and Wright, R.P., 'Second report on Roman buildings at Old Durham' (*Archaeologia Aeliana* 4th Series xxxix 1951)

Heesom, A., *The founding of the University of Durham* (Dean and Chapter of Durham, 1982)

Hutchinson, W., *The History and Antiquities of the County Palatine of Durham* (3 vols., 1823)

Johnson, M., *Durham, Historic and University City* (Turnstone Ventures, 1987)

Mackenzie, E. and Ross, M., *An Historical, Topographical and Descriptive View of the County Palatine of Durham* (Mackenzie and Dent, Newcastle, 1834)

Mee, A., *The King's England: Durham* (Hodder & Stoughton, 1969)

Mills, J.A., *The Story of Bear Park* (Home Words, 1956)

Morris, R.J.B., *The City of Durham, its Town Hall, Guildhall and Civic Traditions* (Town Clerk, Durham, 1990)

Norris, R., *The Stained Glass in Durham Cathedral* (The Dean and Chapter of Durham, 1985)

Pevsner, N. and Williamson, E., *The Buildings of England: County Durham* (Penguin Books, 1983)

Pocock, D. and Norris, R., *A History of County Durham* (Phillimore & Co., 1990)

Proud, K., *Great Northern Saints* (Discovery, 1983)

Proud, K., *The Prince Bishops of Durham* (Keybar, 1990)

Richardson, M., *Britain in Old Photographs – Durham, Cathedral City* (Sutton Publishing, 1997)

Richardson, M.A., *The Local Historian's Table Book, of Remarkable Occurrences, Historical Facts, Traditions, Legendary and Descriptive Ballads &c connected with the counties of Newcastle-upon-Tyne, Northumberland and Durham* (M.A. Richardson, 1846)

Richmond, Romans and Wright, 'A civilian bath-house of the Roman period at Old Durham' (*Archaeologia Aeliana* 4th Series xxii 1944)

Roberts, M., *Durham* (B.T. Batsford Ltd/English Heritage, 1994)

Shea, W., *Carpet Making in Durham City* (Durham County Council, 1984)

Simeon of Durham, *A History of the Church of Durham* (Llanerch Enterprises, 1988)

Smith, D., *The Story of Sanctuary at Durham* (Frank Graham, Newcastle, 1971)

Stranks, C.J., *Durham Cathedral* (Pitkin Pictorials, Andover, 1970)

Stranks, C.J., *The Life and Death of St. Cuthbert* (S.P.C.K., 1987)

Stranks, C.J., *This Sumptuous Church* (S.P.C.K., 1983)

Stranks, C.J., *The Venerable Bede* (S.P.C.K., 1955)

Swanton, M., *The Anglo-Saxon Chronicles* (Phoenix Press, 2000)

Sykes, J., *Local Records or Historical Records of Northumberland and Durham, Newcastle-upon-Tyne and Berwick-upon-Tweed* (1866)

Wall, J., *Durham Cathedral* (J.M. Dent & Sons, 1937)

White, Peter A., *Portrait of County Durham* (Robert Hale, London, 1967)

INDEX

Numbers in **bold** refer to illustration page numbers.

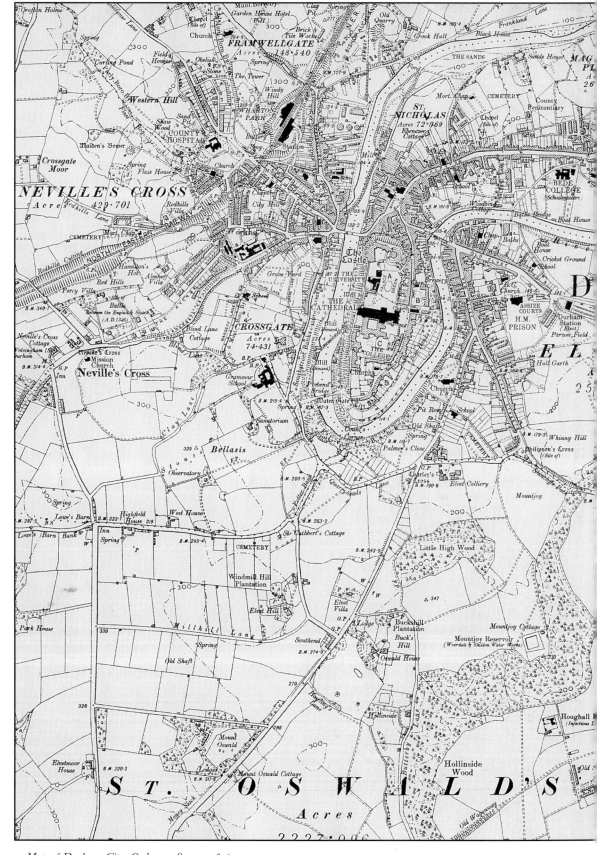

Map of Durham City, Ordnance Survey, 1896